SWING TRADING

The proven strategies for beginners to make profits fast in the market. How to become a successful trader for a living with options and stocks, using money management.

Author Name:

Andrew Steve Hammer

Table of Contents

Introduction 1
Chapter 1: Swing Trading Basics 3
    Advantages of Swing Trading 7
    Disadvantages of Swing Trading 11
    Why Swing Trade? 13
    How to Start Swing Trading (Tips) 15
Chapter 2: What to Swing Trade 21
    Swing Trading Stocks 25
    Swing Trading Options 29
Chapter 3: Swing Trading Tools and Platforms 39
    Swing Trading Software 40
    Swing Trading Indicators 43
    Swing Trading Charts 48
    Swing Trading with Candlesticks and Oscillators 52
    Trading Plan 53
Chapter 4: Technical and Fundamental analysis 55
    Fundamental Analysis 55
        Advantages 59
        Disadvantages 60
    Technical Analysis 61
        Advantages 63
Chapter 5: Strategies for Beginners 73
    Hull Moving Averages 74
    Support and Resistance Strategy 75
    CCI Moving Average Strategy 76
    Channel Trading Strategy 77
    Use of Bollinger Bands 79
    Fibonacci Retracement Strategy 81
    Floor Trading Strategy 83
    Trendline Strategy 84
    Breakout Strategy 86

Chapter 6: Time and Money Management in Swing Trading 89

Swing trading Risks 90
  Market Risks 90
Money Management for Stocks Traders 95
  The Two Percent Rule 96
  Position-Sizing 97
Establishment of Trading Mindset 98
  Definition 99
  Winning Mindsets 99
  How Can You Grow Your Mindset? 103

Chapter 7: Ideal Strategies for Swing Trading Options 107

Why We Choose Options for Swing-Trading 108
  Call-Buy Options 108
Profitability Chart 112
Consider Moving-Averages 113
  a. Simple Moving Average or SMA. 113
  b. Exponential Moving Averages or EMA 113
Float 113
Short Interest 114
Volatility 115
Pullbacks 116
Fibonacci Retracement Indicator 116
Rules of Trading Pullback Strategy 117

Chapter 8: Swing Trading Examples 123
Chapter 9: A Day in the Life of a Swing Trader 135

Swing Trading Goals 135
Swing Trading Objectives 139
Routine of a Swing Trader 141
  Pre-market 141
  Trading Hours 144
  After-market Hours 145

Introduction

Swing trading entails purchasing financial instruments, holding on to them for a short span of time then selling them off at a profit. It is a trading strategy that enables you to generate income from short-term trading strategies. To succeed in swing trading, it is crucial that you know how it works.

Swing trading enables you to take advantage of changes in stock prices, also known as swings to make profit. The strategy presents you with numerous benefits that are missing in both day trading as well as buy and hold investment strategies. You can make profit from both the upward and downward changes in stock prices.

As a swing trader, you can trade several instruments including stocks, options, futures and currencies. This book discusses numerous components of swing trading and teaches you how to swing trade the numerous financial instruments mentioned above. It defines the trading style and outline the basics involved in the trade. It also highlights the advantages and disadvantages of swing trading different types of stocks and options.

The book also provides you information on the tools and platforms necessary for swing trading and highlights the strategies beginners as well as professional traders can employ to succeed in the trade.

As you scan through the book, you will get to understand how to determine entry and exit points for each trade, as well as how to minimize the risks associated with the trade. The book covers all the latest topics associated with swing trading and lists some of the ways you can use to analyze the swing market for the best opportunities. If you read the whole of it, you will master every skill required to excel as a swing trader. Ideally this books is great addition to your library whether you are a new trader or an expert swing trader seeking to diversify your portfolio.

Chapter 1: Swing Trading Basics

Swing trading is a strategy used by traders to generate profit from the stock market over days or weeks. The strategy makes use of technical trading to identify the right opportunities for traders. It also uses fundamental analysis to determine patterns and trends in stock prices.

Traders use this technique to purchase and sell stocks whose prices have a high change potential in future. They make profit from the upward or downward trend of the market. Trades must be completed as fast as possible in order to realize the best profits from swing trading.

Swing trading entails holding trading positions over several trading sessions. However, this only goes on for a number of days, weeks or months. The strategy utilizes short term methods of trading and cannot be applied to long-term trades spanning more than a year. Some of the financial instruments traded using this strategy include commodities, indexes, cryptocurrencies, bonds and stocks.

Technical analysis helps swing traders to identify the kinds of stocks whose price might either increase or decrease in the near future. Traders always analyze the technical indicators available on the market to identify such price movements. This enables them to estimate the right time to purchase or sell positions. As a trader, you main focus should be capitalizing on the price changes, in this case known as swings. Small profits made over time often grow into significant results. For instance, a long-term trader can wait for 6 months to make a profit of %20 from one trade while a swing trader can earn a profit of 5% every week from several trades. In the long run, the swing trader makes a lot more than other traders.

When swing trading, you can make use of daily, weekly or monthly charts to identify the right entry and exit positions for each trade. You can use the strategy on volatile stocks as well as on average ones. Either way, you can still make profit from any slight changes in stock prices. The aim is always to capture some returns from anticipated price movement then moving on to another opportunity.

Swing trading is considered an active form of trading just like day trading. Opportunities are selected based on reward/ risk percentages. These percentages are derived from trading charts. Each chart provides information on two forms of swings – the swing low and the swing high. The swing low occurs when the price of a certain financial instruments assumes a downward trend. The swing high occurs when the price of the instrument assumes an upward trend.

The work of the swing trader is to monitor how the price changes from low to high. When the cost of an instrument starts to increase, the trader makes a purchase from the low price and waits for the price to hit a maximum high to open a sell position. The standard procedure used in swing trading is as follows:

1. You purchase or sell a financial instrument that is trending on the market

2. The cost of the instrument indicates a potential rise or decline based on the necessary technical analysis carried out
3. You sell or purchase the instrument after a few to several days depending on the direction assumed by the market prices
4. You the close the position and repeat the same process using different positions and financial instruments.

The outcome of each swing trade is determined by how the market changes. Some predictions may not be as accurate as indicated by technical analysis tools. That is why you must be flexible when it comes to the outcome of each trade since you can make more or less than what you have anticipated.

There are several similarities between swing trading and day trading. The only difference is about the trading period. Day trading does not involve overnight holds, while swing trading does. A day trader must ensure closure of all positions before the trading day ends. A swing trading position can remain open for days, weeks and even months. The risk involved in swing trading is however larger than day trading because drastic changes to a stock price may occur during the night. Gaps may also occur due to some changes in financial news and this can result in tremendous gains, or losses.

Swing trading is often considered to be a combination of short and long-term trading strategies.

Advantages of Swing Trading

Swing traders often take short positions or long ones depending on the nature of position and the potentiality of the stock to generate profit. The strategy entails several benefits including:

- *Success is celebrated early* - Since swing trades last a few days to a month, it is easy for you to determine the success of the market within a short time. This grants you the opportunity to keep improving your trading plans and strategies until you achieve the right goals. With sound strategies and trading guidelines I place, it becomes easy for you to make profit from the business.
- *Involves few technicalities* – swing trading is associated with a limited number of technicalities. It entails studying short-term trends in stocks prices. The main focus is limited to market movements, patterns and trends. It is does not concentrate on a wide array of factors that determine the changes

taking place on the market. Several fundamental market factors are never put into consideration when engaging in swing trading. Once you understand how to determine future prices of stocks as a swing trader, you are ready to start taking up positions. This limit helps the trader to focus on implementing only the right strategies for success. That is why it is easy for you to excel in this kind of trade.
- Concentrating on price movements and market changes alone also gives you an opportunity to trade with more confidence, and less stress.
- *Can act as a source of income* - Trading on daily, weekly or monthly basis can give you some good cash at the end of each month. As you continue trading, you will be able to estimate the amount of money you will receive at the end of each trading period. Out of this amount, you can take out some amount as your income. You can define the right trading periods depending on how soon you need to claim your income from the market.
- *Time saving* – swing trading is one of the strategies that does not require constant analysis. It is ideal for traders who do not need to spend all their time on the market. Individuals with full time

employment can still engage in the business and become successful at it. Once you have acquired the right knowledge and skills in swing trading, it becomes easy to identify the right opportunities quick enough to seal them. It also becomes simpler when you are entering and exiting trades. Managing your trades therefore requires very little time.

- *Involves limited risks* – this is by far one of the most important benefits of swing trading. By understanding how to set stop losses, you can significantly reduce the risks involved in each swing position. This means that you can enter large positions without worrying about losing all your capital. Since swing trading involves making several trades in a week, you will have your risk spread across several positions.
- *Prolonged trading periods* – swing traders always have enough time at their disposal to maximize profits. Unlike day trading where positions must close at the end of each day, a swing trader can leave positions open for a considerable amount of time. Doing this gives the trader an opportunity to trade at a schedule that is convenient for him.
- Due to these long periods, it is not necessary for you to monitor the market on daily basis. Once you

have the right parameters in place, you can continue doing other activities as you wait for the right time to enter or exit swing positions. Market setups always allow you to benefit from natural changes occurring in the trading platform. You can increase your profits by simply studying market direction and customizing your strategies in favor of these directions.

- *Utilizes simple tools* – swing trading makes use of very simple algorithms and tools. Because the market does not change too fast, the trader can always take his time to analyze positions and carry out the necessary trades. This advantage makes swing trading ideal for everyone since all that is required is a computer, stable internet and some charts. The basic skill used in the trade is having the right knowledge and ability to study market patterns.
- Clear trading terms – swing trading is often based on the market's technical analysis. This means that there are restricted positions and time periods when it comes to the trade. It is often easy to identify trades that might work against you and avoid them. Due to this, you can limit the amount of loss

associated with bad trades as soon as you identify them.

Disadvantages of Swing Trading

Every trading strategy has the positive side and the negative side. Although there are several benefits associated with swing trading, a small number of cons associated with the strategy exist too. However, these are not significant enough to shield you from engaging in swing trading. Here are some of the risks associated with the trade:

- *Limited capital rotation* – when day trading, you can enter and close positions too quickly and this means that you can buy and sell more stocks within a day. When it comes to swing trading, capital is often held in open positions for a while. If you have limited amounts of capital available, you will not be able to open numerous positions at the same time. Engaging in a more profiting trade may always mean that you relinquish some of the already open positions even if such positions have not generated any profits yet.
- *Margin requirements are a challenge* – because swing trading positions remain open for days, margin requirements for each position keep

changing as days go by. The changes result from the swinging stock prices which may sometimes move against your expectations. That explains why swing traders always need to have a lot of cash as capital, and more on standby in case they need to make additions to the initial deposits. These large margins often discourage investors from engaging in the trade.

- *Traders must be conversant with technical analysis* – this may not be an advantage, but it is a limitation to some people. While anyone can study swing trading charts, it becomes difficult for individuals with little knowledge of technical analysis. Such people are always not able to determine entry and exit points on the charts and this results in tremendous losses. Understanding the fundamentals of technical analysis often requires time and discipline. Engaging in the trade without this knowledge is risking your capital.
- *Higher risks* – one other disadvantage of swing trading is the likelihood of huge losses. When stock prices assume a direction that is opposite to the anticipated direction, a loss occurs. If you do not select your positions wisely, you may wake up to shocking price changes the next day. You may not

be able to monitor the market during the night. Thus you may not be able to close some positions in good time and this can result in high risks of your capital. Not every position guarantees positive returns and if you invest a lot of capital on positions you are unsure of you may experience huge magnitudes of loss within a short time period.

From this, you can learn that the disadvantages of swing trading do not match the advantages. Most of the risks associated with the trade can either be minimized or eliminated completely in case the trader identifies the right strategies to use. The trader can always utilize several methods of trading to improve the profit potential of swing markets.

Why Swing Trade?

Swing trading is quite different from ordinary methods of stock trading. The strategy entails two major activities – buying of financial instruments and selling them at a profit. The process used to accomplish these activities is what differentiates this strategy from the rest.

Swing trading depends greatly on the nature of the market. Profit or loss is obtained depending on the decisions you make as a trader. If you make decisions based on wrong trends and timings, your capital gets lost. You must be patient enough to wait for the right time to make moves on the swing market.

The reason why many traders engage in swing trading despite the major risks involved is because most of the trend predictions are always accurate. With a good plan in place, you can easily generate some good profit from the venture.

Swing trading is also ideal for beginners as well as part time traders. The slightly stretched time frame always favors a large number of investors including those with day jobs as well as beginners with little or no information about the trade. Investors who are willing to spend only a limited time on the market can also swing trade successfully.

Another reason why swing trading may be good for you is because it is easy to learn and implement. Actually, the strategy is easier than day trading as well as other forms of trading. Once you understand how the stock market operates, and once you know how to determine market directions, you can easily start trading without any expert guidance.

How to Start Swing Trading (Tips)

If you are seeking to begin swing trading, you may be wondering the kind of steps you need to take. The first concept you need to understand is that swing trading seeks to exploit changes in stock prices. The trade is always profitable to individuals who spend time understand the nitty gritty involved. Let us look at some of the tips that will help you succeed as a new swing trader.

- Know what the trade entails – some people always confuse swing trading and day trading. For swing trading strategies to work for you, you must first establish that indeed you are swing trading, not day trading. As a swing trader, you must not keep monitoring, entering and closing positions constantly since this will turn you into a day trader.
- Use a demo account – before mastering the swing trading process, it is advisable that you start with a demo account. A demo account allows you to learn the trade without using your real cash as capital. You can make a few trades on the demo account as you incorporate some of the tricks you have learnt about swing trading. Once you start winning on

most of the transactions, you can shift to a real account.
- As you continue trading, concentrate on certain types of stocks first. You may think of diversifying through trading different financial instruments at the same time. Doing this may leverage your profits, but it can also increase the chances of losing your money. Start with a few trades and increase the number as time goes.
- Take advantage of both directions of the market. This increases your chances of making a fortune from the trade. Trading on one side results in the loss of some lucrative opportunities. Always remember to set stop losses for each trade.
- Have a simple strategy - the best way to succeed in swing trading is to work using a sound strategy. Swing trading features several simple, as well as sophisticated strategies. When starting to trade, it is important that you use the basic strategies first. You can keep improving on these as you master the trading process. You must always understand that you cannot learn everything about the trade in a single day. That is why it is important to start with the basics and keep building on this with time. Identify a set of strategies that work for you then

apply them on your trades continuously to achieve the best returns.
- Learn to control your emotions – swing trading requires that you make your market moves without involving your emotions. If you do not control your emotions, you may end up making the most serious mistakes. Despite having feelings of worry, frustration or excitement, always stick to your trading plan and strategy.
- Stick to your trading plan – just like any other form of trading, you need a lot of discipline when swing trading. Determine your entry and exit points in advance, and set your stop loss orders in good time. Do not modify these unless it is necessary for your market performance.
- Seek mentorship – getting someone to teach you the secrets of swing trading is a great way to start. A good mentor will take you through the process and give you tips that will help you to save a lot of money and time. It takes less time to learn through a mentor than when you study on your own.
- Ensure you understand market trends – Swing traders utilize several indicators to determine how market prices will shift in future. Indicators enable you to determine price movements. You can use this

information to improve on your profits. When the market assumes an uptrend, it is advisable that you take positions that have assumed that are going up. When the market is declining then you should take positions that are going downward.
- Other than market trends, you should also be able to study charts and identify stock price patterns. A stock's previous performance can help you to easily determine what you should expect in future. You may need to compare different time frames to locate these patterns.
- Exercise patience – this is true for all trading strategies, swing trading included. You must always be patient enough to determine the right entry and exit positions. When you are always in a hurry, you will keep missing out on some good swing trading opportunities. In case your positions end up at a loss, do not get angry. Instead, scan through your strategy to determine what needs to change.

The trade entails a combination of patterns, trends and tools. These components work together to ensure success. Therefore, you should always focus on the bigger picture. Avoid concentrating on a single component. Instead, work using a combination of most or all of them.

Always remember to go with the trend. Do not ignore long-term analysis information since this will help you determine the direction of the market in the long-term. Remember, you can neither control the market nor the prices of stock. It is your responsibility to customize your plans and strategies to suit the market, not the other way round.

Chapter 2: What to Swing Trade

Swing trading is popular amongst many investors. It can be applied to a wide array of financial instruments including currencies, futures, stocks and options. Each of these instruments has its own advantages and disadvantages. It is the only style that utilizes both long-term as well as day trading strategies.

Swing trading is often used by new as well as experienced traders. It carries several benefits that are not easy to ignore. It basically entails monitoring price movements or 'swings' then seeking to make profit from these swings. To do this, you must enter and exit positions at the right time. Swing trading is always less concerned about the fundamental aspects of financial instruments since it is a relatively short-term form of trading.

Since swing trading entails making profit, it is important to choose the right financial instruments to trade. Essentially, there are numerous factors you need to establish before settling on a particular instrument to swing trade. Some of these factors include:

- *Liquidity of the instrument*. Liquidity is the ease with which traders sell and purchase certain financial instruments on the swing market. As a swing trader, you should focus on instruments that feature high liquidity since these are easy to buy and sell.
- *Compatibility with rule-based systems.* Most swing traders always use systems that are rule based to carry out their trades. Such systems allow traders to create more reliable trading signals. As you select a financial instrument, ensure that you can use it on such platforms.
- *Volatility of the instrument*. Volatility is the rate at which the cost or value of a particular security

changes. This can either be a rise or decline in the price. Highly volatile securities are often easier to sell than those with low volatility. However, these are also associated with multiple risk levels. Most long-term investors often avoid stocks that bear large price swings. However, for swing and day traders, such a swing is what causes profits to be realized. You can benefit from upward and downward price swings alike.

- *Alignment to market trends*. The swing market will always assume a bearish or bullish state. It is important to identify financial securities that are capable of moving with these trends. Trading software can assist you in filtering the kind of stocks available for trading to only those that are aligned to the current market trend.
- *Transaction costs.* Different financial instruments feature different trading costs. If you have limited capital, you will need to choose an instrument that requires less cash to trade. Several financial instruments always require very little capital to trade. These include brokerage fees and commissions.
- *Information availability.* Some financial instruments are popular than others. Availability of information is

necessary in case you need to learn about a strategy or skill required to trade a particular stock. For example, if you do not have access to financial news updates relating to a certain financial instrument, it becomes difficult for you to estimate when the prices may change. Therefore, as you choose a financial instrument, make sure that its information is freely accessible.

- *Subject to technical analysis.* Some financial instruments work best with technical analysis while others do not. As you make your choice, ensure that the instrument you select is easy to analyze using technical indicators and patterns. Most swing traders use technical indicators because they are simple, systematic and easy to use. When applied correctly, technical analysis generate the right signals that you can use to enter and exit the swing market.

Beside the few points above, you also need to consider the level of risk associated with the instrument as well as the current market conditions where the instrument can be traded. Because swing trading favors a number of securities, it is easy for you to diversify your investments in a manner that reduces the risks associated with the traded.

Swing Trading Stocks

Stocks are financial securities that indicate ownership of a certain company and its assets. Trading in stocks can get a bit confusing if you do not understand the various types available on the market today. If you are a novice swing trader, getting to understand stocks can take you a lot of time. However for professional stock traders, swing trading stocks is no big deal to them. To trade in stocks, you must specify the level of risk you are ready to tolerate and the amount of time you would like to leave positions open.

There are generally two major types of stocks – preferred stocks and common stocks. Commons stocks are those that are freely available to the public for trading. Most of the stocks available on the market today are of this form. They give you ownership of the company and part of the profits. These are often associated with high profits than other categories of financial instruments.

Preferred stocks on the other hand give you some level of right over a company but not the right to vote. The guidelines associated with preferred stocks always vary from one company to another. In case the company decides to go liquid, owners of preferred stocks are often paid off their share costs before those holding common stocks receive their payment.

Stocks can also be customized depending on certain classes. For instance, there are blue chip stocks which represent shares from large companies that keep experiencing tremendous growth. Traders always prefer such stocks over other classes of stock because the returns are always guaranteed. There is also speculative stocks that represent shares from organizations which have a very undefined financial history. Such stocks always feature high levels of risk since their stability is questionable. Nevertheless, the stocks always bear high profit capabilities and some traders always ignore the risk associated with them.

With growth stocks, the company listing them always has potential for receiving high returns in form of earnings. Such companies always reinvest their earnings back into the business for it to grow. They also pay some dividends to stock owners depending on the number of shares invested. Value stocks are often undervalued, but carry great profit potential. Investors always purchase such stocks with the hope that the price will eventually be revised to a fair one in future. Lastly, penny stocks feature very low prices, low volatility and high risk. These are often avoided by most people because they rarely generate any income.

When trading stocks, you should look for those that have high profit potential and high risk tolerance. When choosing the right stocks to trade in, be sure to check their volume levels. Most swing traders always choose the stocks that are highly liquid. This is because it is easier to close positions associated with high volume stocks faster. Since swing trading requires that you close positions soon enough to realize profit, it is essential that you have liquidity of stock in mind when seeking the right one for the trade. Such stocks also feature lower bid-ask spreads that are favorable for swing trading.

Another aspect you need to have in mind when trading in stocks is the availability of the stock with market makers. These are individuals who hold certain stocks for some time to increase their liquidity and balance the market. Most of them are always paid a small amount for holding the shares. As a swing trader, your focus should be getting such stocks since this will ensure that you are dealing with an instrument that will remain on demand during the entire trading period.

When swing trading a particular stock, check how it correlates with market indices and other categories of stocks. This is because some stocks may seem to have the right trading features, but these end up swinging against the market direction. If you trade in these stocks, you will end up losing a good percentage of your capital. You need to focus on stocks that are volatile enough to cause a price swing. Swing trading becomes irrelevant when you apply the style on stocks whose prices are not moving.

As you get the right stock for swing trading, you want to find out if there are any upcoming activities and events that may affect the stock prices significantly. Such events may be things like release of a new product, or an upcoming earning for the company.

Here are a few quick tips that you can use when swing trading stocks:

- Use both short-term and long-term charts as well as time frames
- Enter the market as soon as a price trends starts and not at the end of it
- Use more than one indicator to analyze the market
- Align your swings with the market direction
- Have a trading plan before you start swing trading
- Master all the aspects of swing trading
- Check out for daily news on the underlying company and industry before entering positions. Also be mindful of general market news such as economic and political news as these can impact stock prices drastically
- Go long when the market is strong and short when the market is weak
- Monitor trends in the market prices and trade in relation to the trend

Swing Trading Options

Options represent derivatives of other financial instruments. Unlike stocks, options do not grant you ownership of the shares of a company. They only grant you the right to either purchase or sell the underlying security at certain trading terms.

Swing trading features several strategies that are applicable in trading options. Although this form of trading is not embraced by many people due to the nature of options, a good number of traders have successfully attempted and succeeded in swing trading options. One major characteristic that makes swing traders avoid trading options is the time decay aspect. As an option approaches expiration, its value tends to diminish. However, with the right swing trading strategies, you can take advantage of price swings to generate some quick profits from options before they expire.

If you decide to swing trade options, you can decide to use payoff or payout profiles to gain more understanding of what a particular contract will pay you off when the option expires. There are basically two kinds of options – call options and put options. Swing trading can be applied to any of these types successfully. You can also utilize some of the options trading orders to create either short positions or long positions depending on the market trend.

You may also decide to maximize profits and reduce risks by running more than one contract simultaneously. This creates what is known as an option spread. Spreads are commonly used in basic options trading to increase profit opportunities and reduce the level of risk. When swing trading options, there are basically two methods you can use. These are mechanical trading and discretionary swing trading.

Mechanical swing trading entails the use of standardized rules to establish entry and exit points on the swing market. You can identify these points manually or through the use of your swing trading software. The second type of swing trading or discretionary trading entails using individual analysis and judgment to make trading decisions. This kind of swing trading is riskier than the first one since it does not help you to control your emotions when trading.

When it comes to swing trading options, it is important for you to establish the right strategies to use. Some strategies that can be effectively used on stocks may not be effective when trading options. You must also understand the kind of chart patterns and trends that need to be used in your transactions. Failure to do this can lead to the loss of your options premium which you would have invested as the trading capital.

You must also specify the level of flexibility with which you wish to trade and have a clearly outlined plan for your business. Options prices are always more unpredictable than stock prices. If you are not certain about how to trade them, it is important that you seek assistance, or carry out the necessary research before attempting to trade. You may decide to start with a demo account until you perfect the skill before trying to trade using your real account. When swing trading options, there are a few steps that you need to follow to ensure you succeed in the business. These are:

1. *Choosing the underlying asset* – this is the very first step towards swing trading options. You start by choosing the right underlying asset for your options. You can do this by first monitoring the kind of assets associated with a particular option then selecting the asset that has a higher chance of giving you some profit. When doing this, look for those assets with a correlation with popular indexes since these are always on high demand. Use technical analysis indictors to make this determination. Underlying assets with an RSI value that is more than 70 are

good for selling, and those with a value that is below 30 are good for purchasing. Watch out for a good risk reward ratio as well.

2. *Determine the market direction* – once you have specified the underlying asset you wish to trade in, it is also good that you also identify the right market direction to apply your swing trading strategy. For instance, if the market has a potential to increase in future, you can consider opening a call option contract to sell an underlying asset. When the market has a possibility of declining, you can consider entering a contract to purchase a put option or sell a call option. Remember to use payoff profiles to determine the profitability or loss levels of each position before entering it.

3. *Set the strike price* – the strike price determines the cost you sell or purchase your options at. The more the strike price of an option, the more it will cost when it is sold or bought. Also the more time available before an option expires, the more costly it becomes. As the option approaches expiration, its price keeps going down.

4. When the strike price is higher than the market price for an option, it is said to be in the money or ITM. When the strike price is equal to the market

price, the option is at the money or ATM. When the strike price is lower than the market price, the option is out of money or OTM. Swing traders always seek to make profit from options that are either in the money or at the money.

5. *Choose the expiration date* – the expiration date determines how long an option will last before it stops being displayed on the swing market. Once the option expires, it is no longer available for any form of trading. When swing trading, you should avoid options that are about to expire. Most of these end up worthless during expiration. You also want to avoid options that have very long expiration periods since these always feature high transaction costs.

6. *Plan to enter the trade* – since you have made all the necessary pre-trade plans, you can now start thinking on how to enter the market. The right entry time is important since it determines the outcome of most of your trades. You can use technical analysis to determine the correct entry point. Start by identifying the market trend then determining the right points to get into the market. Check out for pullback and reversal points as these are great for quick profits. One advantage of swing trading stocks

is that you can end positions and close contracts any time before expiration.

7. *Process your contracts* – when in the market, execute your strategies and plans accordingly. For instance, if the market trend is higher than the strike price, you can purchase an out of the money option. If the market price is lower, you can purchase an out of the money put option. Ensure that you get the right broker for this stage of the business so that you do not lose most of your trades.

When you create positions you need to manage them in a way that ensures you do not risk losing your capital. Keep an eye on the underlying market to ensure that no occurrence influences the prices without your knowledge. Compete with the time decay of each option and exercise options as they approach expiration. Do not wait until it is too late for you to relinquish your positions.

Understand the right time to exit the market. This is because the options market is often associated with unpredictable changes in prices based on several factors besides the value of the underlying instrument.

In order to succeed in swing trading options, you need to have sound analytical skills. These skills will help you avoid making rash decisions which may cost you a lot. Analyze every market opportunity before entering any contracts. Wait for the right time to exit as well. Do not close positions prematurely. If you are unable to identify entry and exit positions you can take advantage of the market swings and wait for the right time.

When swing trading options, you need to note that it is not a must that you trade every day. If you do not identify a suitable opportunity for swing trading, it is essential that you wait until one presents itself even if it means skipping a few days. The right opportunities will ensure that you execute your transactions accurately. Set any maximum losses that you are willing to bear for each trading position.

This will save you from any frustrations should the market assume an unpredicted direction. When you get into a bad position that you are unable to recover, get out of it when it is still too early. Doing this will minimize the amount of loss you incur from the trade. You should also define the amount of profit you expect to receive from each swing trading position.

This will ensure that you stay on the market long enough to ensure the profit is realized. If you are working with a broker, it is essential that you ensure he has solid experience in both swing trading and options trading. If you have limited information about the two styles, you can engage a traditional broker who will not only help you to complete your transactions but will also offer you expert advice on all your trades.

Chapter 3: Swing Trading Tools and Platforms

Swing trading is quite popular. Technological advancements have made it possible for traders to take advantage of the rapid changes in stock market prices. Swing traders make millions of money from the trade every day.

More and more people are taking to swing trading over long-term trading and investment because of the quick profits associated with the strategy. The major aim is always to make some income out of it. The responsibility of identifying opportunities to make money lies with the trader.

Swing trading can be carried out in two categories of markets – bear and bull markets. These two market conditions offer the right environment for swing traders to generate income. Your role as a trader is to establish which positions to enter or exit when the market is bullish and the ones to trade when the market is bearish.

To engage in swing trading, there are several tools and platforms you need to have besides having the right amount of capital. This chapter discusses some of them.

Swing Trading Software

Swing trading software is a set of programs used to accomplish the tasks associated with swing trading. Traders use this kind of software to identify the right swing positions and determine how best to apply certain strategies. The software also proposes the kind of stocks you may need to trade and provides you with the necessary alerts for your open positions.

They also provide you with the right market trend information, thus saving you from manually predicting future market trends. Most traders always prefer to customize their own swing trading system. Such a system always comprises of the following five components:

- *Trading strategies* – the instructions and guidelines outlining how you intend to carry out your trades from start to completion
- *Trading resources* – specific materials necessary for completing your trading positions
- *The trading plan* – this comprises of a set of actions as well as processes that are useful in accomplishing these actions

There are several systems and software available on the market today. If you intend to purchase or develop one, it is important that you understand the qualities you need to look out for. An excellent trading system is one that has been tested to ensure that it works. You can always back-test your system using a demo account before using it on your real account. Another feature of a great system is that it restricts you from carrying out emotional trading. The steps involved in creating a swing trading system are as highlighted below:

- *Acquire the right knowledge*. You may decide to take a swing trading course or engage the services of a

mentor to better understand the technical aspects of swing trading.
- *Select the right swing trading time frame*. As stated earlier, swing trading positions last between days and months. You can choose shorter or longer time frames depending on the amount of time you have for the business. Each time frame always features varying risk levels. Doing this in advance will help you create a system that seeks to manage the risks involved.
- *Select your preferred market.* Swing trading markets are available in a wide range of platforms. The kind of market you select will be determined by how active you intend to be. This can also be influenced by the type of market you wish to trade in.
- *Define your profit targets.* Set these depending on how active you intend to be. If you wish to spend more time on the market then you can state a higher profit target than the person who only intends to trade once in a while.
- *Convert the above points into rules*. These rules will eventually serve as your strategy. You can then apply these rules to your trade, but not before you back-test them. Once you have confirmed that the

rules are effective enough, you can keep using them and revising them as necessary. During the back-testing point, you can implement the rules if they are working or keep revising them if they are not working.

A good system always helps you to identify opportunities easily. Doing this ensures that you invest your capital correctly.

Swing Trading Indicators

Swing traders often purchase positions, hold onto them until the market prices get better then sell them at a profit. This is not an easy exercise. To benefit more from the trade, most traders always prefer to use trading indicators.

Indicators assist you in the analysis of stock markets before you enter positions. These indicators, however, do not work as quickly as you may expect. You will need to exercise some patience while using them. If you are patient enough, these indicators can help you win more trades that you could have won without using them.

Trading indicators do not work in all markets. Most of them yield perfect results in markets where price patterns are stable and predictable. The resultant information from the indicators is only an estimation of future prices but not the accurate result. Let us look at some of the popular indicators used in swing trading:

- *Volume of the instrument* – volume indicators are the most common in all kinds of stock trading. They are the easiest to interpret. However, most swing traders keep ignoring them. These indicators give you information about the availability of certain financial instruments. This information helps you to establish whether you would need to trade in certain instruments in future given that they are more or less liquid.
- The volume indicator allows you to make the right choice of stock type, and shields you from engaging in emotional swing trading. Once you determine the price trends on certain stocks, it is easier to implement your strategy based on these trends. This can result in more wins than losses for your business.
- A good number of traders carry out their transactions without these indicators thus end up losing their capital. Since it takes a while for the indicators to start working, some traders always give up too early into the trade. They therefore end up spending a lot of time analyzing the market

manually. Others keep shifting from one indicator to another, wasting a lot of time as well. As a swing trade, you need to concentrate on the indicator you understand well. This should be one that is easy to learn and implement in your trading positions successfully.

- *Relative Strength Index-* this is a form of technical indicator used to identify positions on the swing trading market. The RSI, as it is commonly referred to gives you the information you need to determine how to enter the market. It works using certain assumptions to create the right signals for your trades. It also helps you to determine whether a particular stock has been overbought or oversold.
- The RSI also indicates whether the market you wish to venture into has trending or stagnant price patterns. These features can always be combined with other market factors such as volume and volatility to identify the right entry and exit points. When a stock is oversold, its cost on the market is less than the actual stock price. This is the right time to buy stock since the price has a potential to change and this can result in tremendous profits. A stock that has been overbought always features a cost that is higher than its actual cost. Individuals

sell their stock at this point since the price is likely to decline in the future. However, most buyers always avoid such stock because of the looming decline in the prices.

- The RSI is always denoted as a figure whose value ranges from 1 to 100. Basically, the relative strength index plays the following roles in swing trading:
- Helps traders to identify those stocks that have either been overbought or oversold. This prepares the trader accordingly and alerts him of the price changes to expect
- Helps you to locate any price divergences that can be used to determine whether or not to expect a reversal in the market trend. You may experience bullish or bearish divergence in swing trading. A bearish divergence takes place when the cost of stock assumes a new highest price which is the same as the SI value. A bullish divergence, on the other hand takes place when the cost of stock assumes a new lowest price that is the same as the RSI. When utilizing this index, you must beware of false signals that result from rapidly occurring swings.

- *Visual analysis* - this works using visible patterns that are easy to understand and interpret. As a trader, you are able to easily view the state of the market and make your swing trading decisions based on this state. How you interpret the information you see from the patterns depends on the level of skill and knowledge you have about swing trading and visual analysis in general.
- *Moving averages* – traders use these averages to identify or confirm a particular market or price trend. One of them is the simple moving average that is easy to use and understand. To use this average, you must provide the closing prices for your choice stock over a given number of days. The indicator then takes the total price and divides with the number of days indicated to obtain the moving average. The other moving average often used in swing trading is the exponential average or EMA.

Generally, moving averages create support and resistance levels for the market which can help a trader determine if the future market will be bullish or bearish. These levels also help you to determine when to trade. For each average, you must learn how it works for it to benefit your trades. In a nutshell, moving averages always serve two major purposes:

- They help you to establish the strength of a particular trend. You can use this information to determine how strong or how weak the market is.
- Moving averages may also signal changes in trend direction. When the market is strong, stock prices are likely to maintain one direction for some time. When the market is weak the prices are likely to change course in future.

Swing Trading Charts

Swing trading is all about trends. One major tool used to establish and analyze trend performance is the swing chart. When used correctly, swing charts often guarantee you some good profits.

In most cases, the charts are used to carry out technical analysis of the market. The charts make the process of studying trends quite simple. Market trends are always at the core of swing trading because traders use them to generate income. These charts always indicate less noise of the market. They keep any confusing information and patterns off and only provide you with the right data that can enable you make sound trading decisions. The charts also give you a great opportunity to utilize other forms of analysis to increase the accuracy of your trades.

There are numerous types of charts used in swing trading. Some are simple and ideal for new traders. Others are a bit complicated and require a more in-depth knowledge of swing trading to use them. Most of these charts are freely available online. It is essential that you select the right charts for your trade.

Most people always prefer free charts over premium ones as long as they serve the purpose. Premium versions always come with a monthly charge. These feature several customizable templates as well as a number of trading indicators. Before choosing any kind of chart, always look at the features possessed by the chart and whether these are compatible with your swing trading strategy.

Some charts exist as standalone applications while others are online based. Great versions also feature community forums where you can interact and share ideas with other swing traders. This aspect of collaboration is very important for beginners since they can get their questions and concerns addressed within no time.

It is always advisable that you choose a chart software that allows you to customize the kind of indicators and templates that you wish to use. All these features must remain compatible with your trading platform and the kind of indicators you wish to feature in your positions. If you will be engaging the services of a broker you may also want to ensure that the chart software can easily connect to your brokerage accounts.

The kind of charts you choose for your business also relates to the time frame you wish to trade in. In relation to the time frame, you may choose daily, weekly or monthly charts depending on your trading periods. When swing trading, it is recommended that you begin with big time frames. This is because you can easily determine the course of such trading positions and adjust your trading prowess accordingly. Large time frames always create a bigger picture of the market trends and this enables you to trade with more confidence.

Large timeframes also need charts that feature large time intervals like weekly and monthly charts. Small timeframes utilize charts with small time intervals like the daily charts to determine market trends. Using these charts, you can easily identify daily and weekly trends which help you understand the direction the stock is likely to take. A strong trend in either direction – that is the upside or downside may indicate a possibility of a pullback occurring in the near future.

You may use charts to locate these pullbacks and make your plans around them. When the market trend looks like it is going to end soon, there is a likelihood that resistance and support levels may form. You need to prepare your strategy for this accordingly.

You can decide to use both daily as well as weekly charts on your swing trading positions. Daily charts are always preferred over weekly charts because they are able to provide trades with information from a more concentrated area of interest. It is easy to determine changing trends in a daily chart than through a weekly chart. The trends established using daily swing charts are known as micro trends and those identified using weekly charts are called overall trends. These terms generally refer to trends either moving upwards or downwards.

When daily charts and weekly charts display the same patterns for the same position, it means that the current trend may continue for a longer time before changing direction. During this time, you can easily place longer trades and still make some profit from them.

When the micro trend assumes a direction that is different from the overall trend, it is an indication that you should enter into shorter positions that are easy to exit. This however, should only last as long as the micro trend is active. Once it ends, you can take advantage of the overall trend and make some longer trades.

Swing Trading with Candlesticks and Oscillators

These two tools are often used in combination or separately depending on what you wish to achieve as a trader. They often indicate the potential of swing trading positions to generate income for the trader. Since swing trading concentrates on short-term changes in prices, candlesticks and oscillators make use of these changes to create revenue.

When analyzing market prices, it is essential that you understand the future direction of the market, as well as the market strength. Oscillators and candlesticks always make this possible. These tools also enable you to identify reversals in market prices. They always pinpoint some conditions necessary for a reversal to take place. When using candlesticks, the reversal is indicated using some indecision candles as well as those that indicate a total change in the market setup. This can be a change from selling of stock to purchasing it, or a change from stock purchasing to selling it.

Oscillator prices may also diverge when the cost of a stock assumes a direction that is opposite to the direction of the oscillator. The stock price always loses momentum right before a reversal occurs. Divergence also becomes slow when a reversal is about to take place. Most reversals are always forecasted using diverging costs. However, there are those which cannot be forecasted with this feature. Sometimes divergence may not occur during the entire trading period. But when it does, be sure of a good trade.

Trading Plan

The tools mentioned above cannot work best if you do not have a plan. A trading plan assists you to organize your daily swing trading activities in a manageable way. The plan outlines some of your trading objectives and ensures that you accomplish every task at the right time. From the plan, you can come up with a routine that works for you. When you have a good plan in place, you will always understand the kind of move you need to make at every point of your trading sessions. It eliminates the use of guesswork, which is always a risky affair. Swing trading discipline always starts with making a plan.

Planning also helps you to adjust your strategies to meet your daily and weekly profit targets. When you study your trading history and understand the kind of changes you need to make in your routines, you will be able to cut your losses by a significant percentage. You can always establish whether your plan is working or not by the outcome of your transactions. If you keep winning in most of your positions, then your plan is highly effective. If you, however, keep losing at each trade, your plan could be the problem. Once you identify some weak points of your trading plan, you can easily make changes to avoid any mistakes in future.

Your plan must always include the necessary trading tools and resources. This includes things like charts, indicators, as well as information about the kind of software you want to use. Ultimately, the tools you choose for your business will determine whether you succeed in the trade or not. Therefore, you need to choose wisely. Take your time to study every aspect of each tool before incorporating it in your plan. With so many options available, you want to ensure that whatever you get leverages your profits and helps you to minimize any risks associated with swing trading.

Chapter 4: Technical and Fundamental analysis

Technical and fundamental analysis are often used in stock trading to provide market information and predict future price performance. Each of these techniques has its own way of operation, advantages as well as disadvantages.

Fundamental Analysis

This method of evaluation and analysis utilizes the intrinsic value of stock to make predictions. It comprises of every aspect of the financial status and economic conditions of certain regions and organizations. Fundamental analysis creates data from aspects such as assets and liabilities, expenses and the income of a company.

Although most researchers have continued to argue against the effectiveness of this method, it has proven to be useful over time, especially in long-term trading strategies. The underlying forces that drive the economy are usually analyzed to establish any new developments in the market. Basically, fundamental analysis entails three major activities:

- Analysis of the entire economy
- Analysis of a particular industry
- Analysis of an organization

Fundamental analysis is a wide concept that brings together various aspects of the market. The resulting data is often combined to identify those stocks that are overvalued and those that may be undervalued. The technique seeks to establish the fair value of a certain financial instrument, then compare this with the current value to determine the future changes in pricing. It is the difference between the market price and the fair price that is used to make any predictions.

Fundamental analysis is also known as trading the news. Other factors that may affect the results of this analysis include growth rates, employment levels, interest levels, trade reports and several other forms of economic data. The process of analyzing information is carried out using three different approaches discussed below:

- Top down analysis. This approach starts with analyzing a wide span of macroeconomic factors before narrowing down to specific aspects of the market. The results of this approach only comprises

of those aspects that offer the trader some high profits
- Bottom up analysis. This approach is the opposite of the top down analysis. It starts with individual components of the market and works upwards to merge these components into one large segment of information
- Interest rates. Fundamental analysis also utilizes interest rates and trade balances to determine future stock prices. When a particular region or country has more than enough stocks to trade, the demand will be high and prices may go high at one point, then reduce drastically.

The role of fundamental analysis is clear – to establish market trends. There are several factors you need to consider before applying this technique to your market analysis. Number one is the amount of profit you wish to make from the trade. When using fundamental analysis, you can make profit from three major ways:

    o From novice traders who are less experienced in the market. These are always at risk of losing their capital because they do not understand how exactly to enter and exit trades. If you apply the right skills and utilize the right systems, it is easy for you to obtain some profit from your fellow traders.

- From listed companies. You can also make profit from established financial institutions whose financial instruments are likely to make huge price moves on the market. In case this happens, you can easily generate some income from the trade.
- From IPOs. Organizations that may be issuing more stock for trade create a platform for you to make profit from the difference between the IPO price and the final trading price. Although such offerings always involve a lot of risk, you can make some good cash from them if you carry out the right form of analysis.

From the three ways listed above, it is clear that fundamental analysis helps you to make money from some of the major players in the stock market. However, the technique is not quite reliable when it comes to making short-term trading decisions. That is why it must be combined with technical analysis. Some investors still use fundamental analysis independently although the results obtained may not be 100 percent effective.

Fundamental analysis focuses on the aspects related to the company selling stocks directly. The process utilizes various tools that concentrate on growth, earning and the overall market performance. These tools work in combination, and base their performance on the assumption that the company in question will trade its stocks at different price levels. The technique also features several advantages and disadvantages as outlined below:

Advantages

- Ideal for long-term trading. Fundamental analysis is essential for long-term trades. It is tailored to study long-term trade patterns and trends. This makes it easy for you to make long-term predictions on the performance and price trends of certain stocks and companies.
- Helps you select the right company. When carried out properly, fundamental analysis can assist you to identify those organizations whose stocks have high profit potential. You will be able to establish the companies whose assets are valuable enough for trading. This information will be presented to you in form of the company's balance sheets, earning potential and market stability. The technique gives

you adequate knowledge of the trading business and makes you familiar with the necessary market drivers essential for your success. It also equips you with the information you need to identify and avoid stocks from weak companies.
- Allows you to choose the right stocks. Stock prices always move depending on a number of factors. When you gain a deep understanding of the market, it is easier for you to identify which industry group to get your stocks from.

Disadvantages

- Fundamental analysis does not consider some of the major technical factors associated with stock markets. The price of stock can be driven by the company's revenue in the long run. However, this is not true for short-term trades such as swing trading and day trading. This means that individuals always continue to trade stocks of particular companies despite the fall in the amount earned by the company over a specific time period.
- Time consuming. Although fundamental analysis plays an essential role in trading, it always needs a lot of time. The models applied in this technique entail several processes that are time-consuming.

This means that the resulting predications may be contrary to the prices at the moment of trading. Also, each method of valuation can only be applied to a specific industry. That only means that for each industry you venture in, you must change the valuation technique in use. By doing this, you will be wasting a lot of time that can be used to grow your trade in other ways.

- The fair value used in fundamental analysis is often derived from assumptions and not real figures. If any change occurs in these assumptions, the resulting figure will automatically become false. Most analysts are aware of this disadvantage. That is why they always incorporate other analytic tools alongside fundamental analysis.

Technical Analysis

Technical analysis is quite different from fundamental analysis. This technique concentrates on predicting future prices based on the activities taking place in the market. Technical analysis does not entail analyzing the underlying company or industry. Some of the major aspects measured using technical analysis include:

- Volume of certain stocks over time
- Historical prices of a particular stock

- Market trends

The aim of carrying out technical analysis is to capitalize on the changes in prices and market patterns to ensure profit.

Technical analysis often assumes that any other factors associated with a particular financial instrument is incorporated into its price. Therefore the intrinsic value of a given stock item is not factored anywhere in the calculations. The method makes use of charts to identify future trends and patterns for particular markets. Some of the approaches used in technical analysis include moving averages, trend lines, support and resistant levels as well as momentum indicators.

As a technical analyst, you must learn to utilize charts to establish potential profit making opportunities. Traders that use this method always believe that stock prices tend to form patterns known as trends. These trends keep recurring as the market changes. The technique works based on several other assumptions which are:

- The cost of each financial instrument contains all the fundamental economic aspects of the market
- The events and occurrences in the financial market such as changes in interest rates, financial news

updates are also automatically included in the stock price
- Stock price history keeps repeating itself

Technical analysis is commonly used in various financial instruments such as equity, forex and commodity trading. Unlike fundamental analysis that is ideal for long-term trading, technical analysis suits both short and long term trading procedures. Most traders utilize this concept to make good profits from stable markets. Several advantages are associated with this technique. A few disadvantages exist too. Let us discuss some of them.

Advantages

Technical analysis is very popular amongst swing traders and other short-term traders. The technique provides traders with exit and entry points for their trades, which is not the case with fundamental analysis.

- Technical analysis provides the trader with all the necessary information about the current market. The stock price always depicts some characteristics of the market and the underlying company. Stock prices may either increase or decrease depending on the factors surrounding the market. The price acts as a central point where information about the trade can be obtained. As traders keep switching from buying to selling of stock, the price keeps changing.

Technical analysis is able to tabulate these changes in a chart that can help you establish future moves quickly. When using these charts, you can easily find out more information about the market without first establishing why prices keep changing the way they do. Your only focus becomes making money from these changes. That is why trading using technical analysis is easier than when using fundamental analysis. Your main concern is the changes taking place on the charts. You do not waste time interpreting balance sheets or other financial statements. You also don't have to follow any financial news items since the assumption is that all this information is factored in the stock price.

- Easy to establish trends. When analyzing the market using technical data, how the prices change is very important. The good thing is that in most cases the price change forms a predictable trend. Traders take advantage of these trends, which can occur either in the upward or downward direction.

Besides identifying trends, technical analysis also seeks to establish whether the trend is performing well. For instance you can use the technique to locate trends that are not in place, known as sideways markets or corrections. You can also establish when a particular trend is about to reverse.

As a trader, your role in this case is to identify a trend, then enter positions that offer great opportunities within the same trend. Trends always take place at various levels or percentages. For instance, the market may assume an uptrend for a long time or a shorter time depending on the price changes. You need to maximize your profits during this time and technical analysis enables you to do exactly that.

- You can predict future prices from historical price data. Technical analysis is commonly used to identify repetitive activities in stock prices. Sometimes, historical price patterns tend to repeat themselves. At other times, the prices may assume a breakout that is totally different from the previous patterns. Therefore, it is not guaranteed that historical stock patterns will keep repeating themselves.

Technical analysts who understand how stock prices keep repeating take advantage of this to make some good income from the market. One benefit of using historical data is that it shields the trader from playing out emotions when trading. Analysts often study trade charts as a way of identifying any recurring patterns that may be of benefit.

- Saves time. One major advantage of technical analysis is that it does not waste a lot of time on sophisticated model. You are able to time all your trades and establish how best to enter and exit the market. Fundamental analysis requires that you carry out extensive research before making your trades. Technical analysis, on the other hand, allows you to wait for the right time to invest your capital in the trade. What most traders do is that they invest their cash in other trades as they wait for the market prices to get more favorable for trading.
- Flexibility of the technique. Another major advantage of technical analysis is that you can apply the concept to diverse markets. You may easily use it on stocks, futures, options, CFD and real estate.

Technical analysis is also compatible with several other financial instruments. Trading is often tied to some patterns and activities that are displayed in trading charts. You do not need to analyze the market manually to get the right direction to date.

Technical analysis also works for any time frame. It is ideal for short as well as long time frames. You can trade using daily, weekly or even monthly charts depending on the duration of your positions. The patterns and trends displayed on these charts can be translated to small scales for short term trading and larger scales in the case of long-term trading. The approaches used in the technique can easily be applied to different time stretches and still provide the same level of effectiveness.

- Clear entry and exit points. This has already been discussed before. Timing is very essential in stock trading. Technical analysis ensures that you identify the right time to open and close market positions as a way of making profits. This is made possible through the use of tools such as candlesticks, chart patterns and other indicators.

Besides these points, the technique always gives you the right signals for entering and exiting the market. You can always watch out for these signals as they will help you to respond to the market demands accordingly. Analysis of the price and volume of trades will give you an indication of when to trade and when to stay off the market. When a trend is about to reverse, technical analysis will send you a signal in time to prepare you for the price change.

- Less cost incurred. Technical analysis takes place faster than other forms of analysis. The charts are always available free of charge online. Other good ones must be purchased from the companies providing them. If you are a trader that needs to use 1 minute, 30 minutes or 1 hour charts, you will still enjoy great results using this method of analysis.
- Carries lots of information. Although technical analysis does not involve a lot of activities for the trader, it provides all the information necessary for each trading position. The information is excellent enough to drive all categories of trading including day trading, swing trading as well as long-term trading. as a trader, you gain success to information such as market volatility and momentum, support and resistance levels as well as repetitive market

trends. All this information can be found in a single chart.

Disadvantages

In case you intend to use technical analysis in your trades, it is essential that you understand some of the disadvantages associated with the technique:

- Technical analysis sometimes sends mixed signals. For instance, you may find one indicator giving you a sell signal while another one indicating a buy signal. This can confuse you as a trader. That is why most traders combine technical several technical indicators in one position.

    Also, technical analysis is often used to predict stock prices. Traders use technical indicators to identify entry and exit points. However, these points are not always 100 percent accurate since the stock prices may change drastically during the trading period.

- Differences in opinions. When it comes to stock trading using technical analysis, different analysts may have different opinions of the same market. Also, the techniques used to analyze stocks may vary from trader to trader resulting in diverse outcomes.

Eventually, this results in information noise since each analyst tends to believe what they have experienced from the market. When you change your trading schedule even by a few minutes, you will be surprised at the drastic changes that will take place in the outcome of your trades. Sometimes, the signals you receive instructing you to enter or exit the market are fake signals that can only be identified when using large time frames. In case you are engaging in short-term trading, these fake signals can cause you to enter the wrong markets. Doing this will lead to loss of capital to positions you thought had a high profit potential. Most traders seek to boost the accuracy of technical signals by using several indicators at once.

Different traders always interpret technical analysis data differently as well. A trader may sometimes interpret the information in a negative way. Such a trader will apply the information on his trades and may experience tremendous loss. With the market trends and prices that keep changing all the time, sometimes it get difficult to establish whether an analyst has interpreted technical information correctly or not.

Technical analysis figures may fail to produce 100 percent results, but they play a big role in ensuring you understand how to apply your strategies to the stock market. Sometimes, external factors such as the liquidity of stock and company earnings may work better, but in most cases you will find that technical analysis improves your trades more than these factors.

In conclusion, technical analysis is one of the most popular tools among short-term traders. Fundamental analysis is common in long-term trades requiring a lot of time to complete. You can apply these two methods in the kind of market and timeframe you wish. You can easily identify trending periods as well as non-trending periods on the market. How you interpret the information you obtain from technical and fundamental analysis procedures determines the level of success you experience on the stock market.

Chapter 5: Strategies for Beginners

When you are new to swing trading, there are some basic information, tools and strategies you need to understand before getting started. By definition, swing trading strategies are instructions that enable you to enter sell position when the price of stock is bound to turn down, or buy stock when its price is likely to go up. Essentially, these strategies enable you to buy and sell at the right time.

A swing trading strategy must not be sophisticated for it to work. Mostly, complicated strategies always lead to frustration and inconsistent results. There are several strategies that you can use to make the most out of this short-term form of trade. One major advantage of swing trading is that it comprises of a wide array of trading strategies. Some of the factors you need to consider when selecting the right strategy for your startup trade include:

- The type of stock you wish to trade
- The duration of your positions
- The platform you intend to use
- Amount of your target profit

The strategies are made to assist you make the most out of your trading experience. They minimize the risks associated with swing trading while ensuring that you get maximum returns. Here are some of them.

Hull Moving Averages

This strategy can be used by both new traders as well as experts in the industry. It works using the hull moving average indicator that features very fast market information processing capabilities. The indicator is designed in a way that responds to any changes in stock prices.

The HMA strategy helps you to purchase and sell stocks in the swing market using the following two ways:

- *Slope change* – whenever there is a change of slope, the indicator signals you to prepare for a purchase or sale of stock. When the price of stock assumes an upward trend then you should ready yourself to purchase stock. Once the slope assumes a downward trend, you need to prepare to sell the stock in your possession.
- *HMA crossovers* – this method combines two moving averages and crossovers. If the fastest moving average crosses the slower one on an uptrend, you should prepare to sell and when the same occurs on

the downside then the market has assumed a downward trend and you should prepare to sell your positions. Typically, traders always wait for the crossover to take place so that they can place their orders accordingly.

Support and Resistance Strategy

Support and resistance levels are common in swing markets that utilize technical analysis to analyze market trends. These are often represented as lines in technical charts. Support levels are areas on the chart whose cost is less than the present stock price. Resistance levels are points on the chart whose cost is higher than the current stock price.

When the price of stock rises beyond the support area it becomes a resistance area. When the price of stock falls beyond the resistance level, the area becomes a support area. You need to take advantage of these changes to make profit from different market directions. If you wish to use the strategy, you must first understand how to establish support and resistance areas. Once you do this, it becomes easy for you to apply the strategy to your new trades. Besides identifying these areas, you also need to learn how to interpret signals associated with these strategy so that you do not miss any entry and exit positions.

Resistance and support levels in swing trading always occur depending on the level of demand and supply for a particular stock. When demand is high, support levels are likely to occur. The opposite is true for high supply levels. Resistance and support are often marked using swing lows and highs. A swing high is the highest price assumed by a particular stock over a specific period. A swing low is the lowest price of stock for a given period.

CCI Moving Average Strategy

This is another strategy that you can easily adopt as a beginner. CCI stands for commodity channel index. The logic behind this strategy is the identification of future market trends while also checking for overbought or oversold stocks. The trading chart used for this strategy always displays several moving averages as well as a CCI indicator. The moving averages are responsible for determining market trends while the CCI oscillator determines stock performance on the current market.

One advantage of this strategy is that it helps you to understand when to trade, and the right stocks to trade as well. The strategy also applies to diverse timeframes.

Channel Trading Strategy

Channel trading refers to a strategy that helps you identify and trade on stocks with a stronger market trend. These stocks are always a target of most swing traders because they feature a high profit potential. A channel is an area on the stock chart where the price fluctuations remain confined between two parallel trend lines.

The strategy entails identifying bearish or bullish channel trends then entering relevant positions. In case the channel has a trend that is bearish, this becomes the right time to sell your positions. Channels provide a more reliable strategy than many others, yet they remain to be less popular because of the complicated processes involved. They use technical indicators to help you determine entry and exit positions for the swing market. They also reduce the risk of losing capital significantly since you are only able to trade basing on the market direction.

As stated earlier, channels occur between two trend lines. The top line always indicates the stocks swing high while the bottom line connects to the stocks swing low. In case the price of stock rises beyond the top line, then there is a possibility of traders purchasing the stock more. If the price declines beyond the bottom line, more traders could start selling the stock in the near future.

As you seek to begin swing trading, you need to note that this strategy applies well to mid-volatile stocks. If you apply it to stocks that are less volatile, you will only experience minute profits. Highly volatile stocks will generate large profits but also come with high levels of risk.

So, how do you identify channels on your swing trading charts? The first step in using this strategy involves identifying the right channels. A channel is often represented as four price points. There are two lower prices and two high prices that are intertwined. You can identify these manually, with the use of specialized trading software or by use of third party applications.

There are three types of channels:

- Ascending channels that represent rising stock prices
- Descending channels that face downwards
- Horizontal channels represent markets whose stock prices are in stagnation

When using the strategy, always enter a long or exit a short position when the cost of stock reaches the upper trendline. If the price is equal to the lower trendline then you should exit short positions and enter long positions. You should not make any transactions when the stock price is in the middle of the channel.

The channel stops existing when the stock prices rises beyond the top line or falls below the bottom line. At this point, you should also stop trading until another channel forms around the current stock price. You can combine channel trading with other trading strategies to ensure more effective trades.

Use of Bollinger Bands

Bollinger bands are technical analysis indicators used in most forms of trading, including swing trading. The reason why you need to use this strategy is that it helps you determine the probability of stock prices changing. The strategy comprises of three curves that are derived from moving averages. The curve in the middle of the band represents the moving average of stock while the lower and upper curves are derivatives of the middle band.

When the stock price rises beyond the upper band, the stock is said to have been overbought. If the price falls below the bottom curve, the stock is said to be oversold. These work the same way as resistance and support levels. The only difference is that the Bollinger strategy features three points instead of two. Basically, these bands offer you a wide array of trading information including:

- Consolidation periods for the swing market
- Possibilities of reversing market trends
- Upcoming price breakouts in the market
- Price targets as well as potential swing highs and swing lows

When the market has stocks with high volatility, the distance between the three Bollinger bands tends to grow wide. When the market has less volatile stocks, the bands get closer to each other. You can use this attribute to determine which stocks to swing trade for a good profit.

One advantage of Bollinger bands is that they can be used in any particular market and with any financial instrument. One example of this strategy is the middle Bollinger band strategy which instructs you to enter positions as soon as the stock price starts to deviate from the middle band. Majorly, you should buy stock when the Bollinger band is pointing upwards then sell when the band is pointing downward.

In this strategy, your stop loss should be placed at the lower band. To enter a short position:

- Wait for the band to point downward
- Monitor the stock price until it touchers the middle band
- As soon as this happens, sell your positions immediately

When it comes to selling stock, you need to place the stop order at the top band. This strategy is very easy for you to use if you are a new swing trader. However, you need to stop trading when the band size reduces since this is often associated with false signals. Bollinger bands allow traders to create small stop losses even on large positions. This ensures that you gain more on your positions. You can also incorporate candlesticks to this strategy to increase your probability of success. One drawback of this method is that it does not work well on non-trending stocks.

Fibonacci Retracement Strategy

The Fibonacci strategy helps you to identify price reversal points on the swing market. It works through some charts which allow you to plot price performance to identify reversal points.

This strategy was established by Leonardo Fibonacci and has been in use for several decades. It utilizes a sequence of numbers to establish future stock prices. Subsequent numbers are often added together to derive the next number in the sequence. When using the strategy, you are expected to assume that the stock market will always backtrack for some time before completely changing direction. This backtracking is often plotted on the Fibonacci chart so that the trader does not miss out on the reversing point. The plotted patterns are then used to come up with a grid which features swing highs and lows for a given stock. You can use your trading software or other third party apps to draw the grid.

Once you have drawn the grid, you can then use it to identify support and resistance levels for better trading.

Just like Bollinger bands, this strategy works well when applied on trending markets. It does not produce accurate results when used in non-trending markets. Support and resistance levels can only be established when the stock prices keep changing. Several advantages are associated with this strategy when used in swing trading. These are:

- It is easy to use and does not need a lot of indicators to generate accurate results
- Works on both upward and downward swings
- The ability to identify swing reversals offers a great opportunity to make profit

The only downside of this strategy is that it is slow. It takes a considerable amount of time to track price movements. This means that you cannot use it if you are seeking to make quick profits from swing trading.

Floor Trading Strategy

This is one of the simplest and most effective strategies for new swing traders. It involves the use of two exponential moving averages which need to form a crossover for you to trade.

The strategy was originally created for swing traders but was later customized for other trading styles as well. Although the technique works for all time frames, some distortion of signals may occur when it is applied to significantly small time frames. Its aim is to identify price retracements, or price action patterns taking place in the swing market. When the market assumes a downward trend, the price of stock may reduce in stair format, making some swings as it goes down. At this interval, you may also identify some uptrends although the price is fluctuating downwards. These are called retracements. The same also happens when the market starts uprising.

To use this strategy, you first need to establish your trading timeframe. These can be varying depending on the number of trades you wish to run concurrently. You can choose between hourly, daily or weekly charts. Once this is done, you need to wait until the two EMAs cross before placing your trades.

Trendline Strategy

The trendline strategy is also one of the easiest to apply on your new swing trading account. This enable you to make purchases when the prices are low and sell stocks when the prices are at their peak. The strategy involves drawing lines on swing trading charts then waiting for the stock value to reach these lines, also known as trendlines.

Once the price assumes the trendline amount, you can buy or sell depending on whether the market is bearish or bullish. To get started with this strategy, you must first learn how to draw accurate trendlines.

To create these lines, you need to identify two swing lows and two swing highs. The low prices are joined to form the downward trendline while the swing highs are joined to form the upward trendline. You buy or sell stock when its price hits these price peaks. Some of the advantages of this strategy include:

- High risk/ reward ratio due to the use of trendlines
- Profit is generated from the price movements alone
- When you set the stop orders correctly, you can maximize profits by buying at the bottom of the swing and selling at the top of the swing.

One drawback of this strategy is that the prices can break beyond the trendlines before you make any profit from it. Sometimes, the price may fail to touch the trendlines completely. This means that you may fail to realize your target profits from the trade. As you trade, you are expected to sell stock when the market price hits the highest swing price and buy stock when the price declines to the lowest swing price.

When using this strategy, you are required to exit the market as soon as you identify potential for price reversals

Breakout Strategy

The breakout strategy entails taking trade positions early enough before the current trend changes course. As a new trader, your responsibility is to establish points where the stock price is almost breaking out of range. This is often represented by broken support and resistance lines. It can also occur at swing high and swing low positions.

When using the breakout strategy, the idea is to enter the market once the stock prices go beyond certain limits, especially if this is accompanied by increase in stock volume. To apply this strategy in your trades you must know how to determine the strength of the market. This will help you establish whether the volume of stock is changing at breakout or not.

Applying these strategies as a beginner may be difficult at the start. However, the more you use them, the easier they become. The main goal of using these strategies is to increase your chances of making profit from your swing trading positions. A good strategy is one that allows you to choose the kid of stocks and markets you wish to trade in with ease. To ensure success of your trades when using swing trading strategies you need to:

- *Establish the stock price and market trends early enough*. Understanding the kind of market you are trading in (whether it is bearish or bullish) can help you select the right strategy to apply.
- *Trade quickly.* Since stock prices do not remain constant, it is crucial that you enter and close positions fast enough so as to get the right amount of profit. However, this does not mean that you should ignore any technical information you need. Only make transactions when the right market environment has been assumed.
- *Check out for any reversals on the market.* Monitor resistance levels, swing highs and lows and any other chart features to establish points that grant you the best profits.
- *Choose the right stock and the right industry*. The type of stock you select determines how the strategy will work for you. For instance, if you wish to enter into short-term positions that offer quick returns, you may need to select stocks that are highly volatile, as well as those that feature large volumes. The direction of stock prices does not matter in this case, however you must avoid stocks whose prices are not moving at all since these rarely feature any swings.

Also, ensure that you enter the right market. Good markets offer the best environments and tools for trading. Markets that have limited types of stocks may not be ideal for you if you are seeking to diversify your portfolio.

As you continue learning more about swing trading, you may eventually decide to come up with your own strategies based on your level of understanding when it comes to swing trading. You can choose one or a combination of the strategies discussed above and use this to tweak a strategy that is unique to your trading style.

Once you establish that a strategy is not yielding the right caliber of results, you can either revise it or replace it with a more advanced strategy. Always remember that for any of these strategies to work, you must learn to interpret swing charts. Most of the strategies require the use of these charts. If you do not master how to use them, you may get frustrated along the way as you trade.

Chapter 6: Time and Money Management in Swing Trading

Swing trading and time are relatives. You cannot mention swing trading and fail to mention time. Right from the definition, swing trading is the holding of a given instrument over a period of time, usually from overnight to a fortnight. You see, it's all about time.

So time management is very crucial in swing trading because it is one of the limiting as well as determining factors to the trade.

The objective of holding on an instrument is to observe the shifting in price levels as opposed to the days' trading. Because of following greater price shifts and ranges, you must calculate the positions and their sizes in order to limit the downtrend risks.

For you to achieve all these, you are supposed to do a technical analysis to recognize instruments that have short term price force. This trade, in most cases, is done by individuals who have much time to follow up with trends. Large institutions, however, do trade mostly in large-sized securities that do not call for easy entry and exit.

Swing trading Risks

There are various risks associated with swing trading. These are stepping stones that need to be revisited for the better returns to be achieved.

Market Risks

It is easy to lose money. Even if some people or traders have taken it so lightly, it hurts most where your finances are involved. In every speculation of markets, lessons are ever learned the hardest way possible.

On the other hand, margin trading and leverage are some of the profound causes of money loss. It digs deep to your initial capital.

· *Time*

In swing trading, time is a very crucial factor. As for longer-term trading strategies, you can measure your trade over some factors that can only work with time. But as for swing trading, you need consistent monitoring due to its nature of the short term.

It takes up much of your time to monitor the movement of the trend as you weigh it against other factors like price changes. Therefore it is not easy to mix swing trading with other day jobs.

· *Taxes*

As a swing trader, you need to pay taxes as well. If you do not pay your taxes, especially in the United States, you will be caught up by the trading laws. Always ensure that you meet all your financial obligations and liabilities.

· *Risk Management*

It doesn't matter if your interest is in penny stocks or algorithmic services when you do not observe money and risk management strategies, you could suffer losses. Risk must be respected. If you ignore risks, they will take you by surprise.

- *Psychology*

If you are ever in love with fast-moving trades and most dynamic; or are you so intolerant with a requirement to know your fate of being right or wrong immediately, then you possess a right mindset required to be a rich man and swing trade master.

Sometimes, you may employ a strategy that isn't working for you; what do you do? These are the tips to consider solving that question.

The above mentioned are the major rules which govern swing trading. It is upon these rules that you can weigh your objectives to see if your vision is still true.

a. *Plan And Stick To Your Plan*

As the nature of the markets, you expect high and lows. It is better if you allowed the pen and paper to evaluate those ups and downs instead of extending it to your emotions. Sometimes you may be so quick in reacting especially to sell off your stock suppose they do not trend well across then week.

It is, therefore, better if there was some well-set plan to guide you in running your business.

b. Fight Fear By Limiting Risks

People react to fear or risk in different ways. It is good, therefore to define risk parameter which suits your situation. At times you may not be willing, to begin with, a capital of say more than 2 percent of your trading account on just one trade.

You cannot wait for a mentor to educate you on this issue. It is easy to get to know this with time.

c. Think About Long Term Trade.

Many traders are usually obsessed with the last or the upcoming trades. It is, however, good to take it easy if you lost it on your first trial. You need to focus on the long term goal or future expectation. It was once said that: if you personalize losses, you won't trade.

There are survival tips that every swing trader need to know in order to avoid unnecessary loses and further mistakes.

· *Make good use of the news*

As a swing trader, you need enough information on ways on how to limit risks and losses in order to maximize profits.

News events are moving markets today. There are many sites which do the analysis of the markets and general finances by use of price actions, volumes, and charting materials.

If you like information, you could easily tap into such for prospective options and perhaps dividend stocks. You can easily organize your entries and exits appropriately.

· *Make Learning Part Of You*

If you wish to excel in trading, you should yearn for more knowledge and information. Trading information is available all over for those who need it to make diversifies strategies from it.

There is libraries trading information on the internet, and even other sites offer interactive platforms just to provide more information on trading strategies and potential plans. The information ranges from written literature to video tutorials for you to study.

You can easily go through MT4 indicators platform and possible daily alert settings.

· *Establish a Best And Right Broker*

Not all traders have common needs and priorities. Different platforms are available for different traders by different brokers. You need to do research on which broker best will suit your personal needs.

There are also various places where you can get quotes and exchange your securities, so its the work of the brokers to find for you the right place to do so.

· *You Need A Journal*

Perhaps an excel journal will do for you. Things like prices, markets rates, dates, positions or sizes, entry and exit reasons etc. are some of the issues that require a warm record for future reference.

Furthermore, it could help you to view your plans for pairs of currencies which do not work on given plans like weekly etc.

Money Management for Stocks Traders

As a swing trader, you need to have a strong yet flexible money management strategy to help govern your finances. It is not so easy to control the market; however, you can only control your finances and the potential risks that come with your trades.

It was said by William O'Neill that, secrete to win for a stocks market, is to lose the very least amount possible when you are not right.

If you have a well-established money management strategy, it will be able to respond to such queries as:

- What is the right amount of money that needs to be risked on a given trade?
- How many shares are supposed to be bought?

A firm trading strategy will remain invalid as long as it has no money management plan. If you admire trading stocks or would like to gain much from the markets, then you need to embrace a smart money management plan.

The most important aspect as a swing trader is to maintain your capital for long to alive and active and watch other winners cover your costs of losing trades and to make some profits. This can only be achieved through a reasonable money management strategy.

The Two Percent Rule

It is true to most swing traders that you do not need to risk more than two percent of your capital one trade. As you know, the stocks market is usually random in nature, and this is the plain truth.

Whatever the case, even as for good charts, chances are that the stock won't go in your expected direction; hence you will end up losing money on such a trade. Ask yourself how much money you would lose suppose this happened?

Confirm the total amount of money on your accounts every first or a new month. Assume you have a total of say $10,000 on your account. Two percent of this amount will be $200. Now this will be the amount you stand to lose on a trade.

Position-Sizing

Assume you are working with a stock which has pulled thus trading at $20.00. Because it looks like it may reverse, you, therefore, decide to go for it. It is wise to speculate where your stop shall be placed. You need to think about how much of your money you may lose rather than imagining of making profits.

Assume that your stop is resting on $19.00. When you buy stocks at $20.00, when your stop s placed at $19.00, it means that your risk is $1.00/share. You can purchase the number of shares equivalent to the risk amount like in this case $200.

The reason is if you do not purchase this amount, then you risk losing the$200 of your shares which is actually the most amounts you are eligible to lose. In this instance, the real number of shares which you need to purchase should be less due to commissions and slippages which you need to account for,

When you manage your money well on all trades, it is easy to refresh because all losses incurred as a result may remain insignificant to your accounts. It also gives many traders some rest from emotional stresses.

In case you get a loss once, you will breathe in and out and continue with other trades, but if you have a series of losses, then sit down, reevaluate the possible causes and even reduce the size of the position to 1 percent.

You Need A Money Management Calculator

This is a written program that helps you to calculate your finances to determine how best you would wish to invest. If everything sounds funny, what you need here is a money management calculator. You need to establish the right calculator that suits your needs.

Establishment of Trading Mindset

When you do not have the right trading mindset, the chances are that you might fail terribly. This is the greatest aspect that any trader posses. You need to work on your trading mindset long before you even think about beginning the real business or its strategies.

If you have a positive mindset, it is an asset; you should work on maintaining and preserving it at all times as long you are still a trader.

Definition

Mindset is a well-established attitude that is held by any individual. This tells us that we need to have a set of attitudes which will govern the way we trade for us to be successful.

Winning Mindsets

Successful trading is not very easy because the development of the right attitude is also the way of developing habits and necessary skills for profitable trades.

This is attributed to resistance in everything, including trading. In whatever sector you are in, you will always have the top 10 as well as top 10 and the intermediate. If you have the best mindset, you can easily climb the ladder to the top.

How to Identify the Right Beliefs and Attitudes

Identifications of the right beliefs and attitudes are the basic process for any successful trading process. There are a number of factors to consider when selecting the right mindsets as below:

1. The Need For commitment

At all costs, you must remain committed to whatever task assigned to you and not quitting and that you can apply every necessary mechanism to achieve the set goals. It entails working to develop the right mindset and not just the trading skills alone.

2. The Need For Persistence

If you have to be a most profit-making trader, and maintaining of that mindset of winning in trading is not as easy as it is said. You need to tune yourself to be flexible yet fluent in moving up and down to ensure that you excel even during financial hiccupping.

3. You Need Self Awareness

For you to develop a winning mindset, you need to re-examine yourself. When you find yourself being critical or emotionally judgmental when things are not right, you need to reassess yourself. Instead, you need to stay put and acknowledge them and therefore come up with an action plan that will build and strengthen your areas of weakness.

4. Performance Metrics.

You need to know if you are growing or not. You have to come up with measures that will help you test your performance metrics against your goals. You need to evaluate the results of the set goals regularly. You need to ensure that you are accountable for those results.

Persistence comes in at this level. You need to persist in analyzing your performance metrics against set goals and set measures to improve.

5. Positive-Attitude

The truth must be told. If you have a positive attitude, you will always stick on the truth and not malingering with lies. N this case, when you notice that something isn't right, you will not pretend that it is good, but instead, you will go ahead to correct the situation.

You agree with yourself that I did not perform so well. But next time I will work very hard to balance the equation. It is the very opposite where someone will see something wrong but goes ahead to acknowledge that it is good. This habit is characterized by failures and not winners. You will never grow with this type of attitude.

6. You Need To Have Hunger

This is not the hunger for achieving much but the hunger for growth. A mindset for growth will usually stick to the correct pathway with continued improvement. This is the right hunger for every trader because, if you grow in your abilities, it is easier to achieve much financial empowerment than if you decide to be young in trade.

7. Humility

A person that has a winning trading mindset is not any smatter pr better off than anyone else whatsoever. Instead, he acknowledges that growth is a difficult process that needs humbleness or else remains static or even decline further.

8. The Spirit Of Openness

It is impossible to share out our mistake and errors and more so for those people who are at leadership levels. When you opt to share your struggles which can attract some support from others, it will make you grow steadily.

Sometimes, there we grow as a result of our most difficult situations that were shared with others who at the end, gave us some guidance and advice on how to improve on them.

Remember that as much as we are not willing to share our difficult moments with others for help, even others have gone through such and come out more successful than before.

The Battle is in Your-Mind.

As a trader, having a successful mindset only won't do anything to improve your trading outcome. What you need to understand is that the right mindset should be combined with the right actions for you to achieve great returns.

Many people talk of success as a result of a positive attitude. That is not the case. The truth lies in the fact that a rightful mindset is just a catalyst for growth. When you have no right attitude, the chances are that, as a trader, you will move on the right journey success.

Attitude precedes actions and then come results as the cycle moves on. This can be called the growth cycle.

How Can You Grow Your Mindset?

This is a question that you need to ask yourself. Are you are growing your mindset towards developing your trading skills. You need to come up with a questionnaire comprising of possible questions that you need to tick either right or false and keep on to ensure that it helps you to grow.

You need to be committed to what you are doing and be persistent to achieve good results. As times goes by, you need to continue responding to the questions that you set. This is one way of enhancing self-awareness.

You need to take some good time to reevaluate your traders' mindset to see if you achieve much or not.

If you are true to yourself, the chances are that you will be able to find as many areas in your life that need improvement as possible. This is turn becomes one of the success factors in establishing a true and successful trader mindset.

If you get this concept down to your mind, you will achieve a lot; you will be able to apply it by drawing your trading strategies and other workable tactics, tools as well as skills. However, the mindset will remain the key feature for every successful trader, and nothing changes from that.

In conclusion, we have talked much about the mindset as the key driver for one's realization of potential trading ability. If you have the right mindset, you are good to go. You will be able to grow drastically in the knowledge and skill as a swing trader.

We have been able to consider the right trading mindset as one that aims at taking advantage of learning new things and not bragging on past successes. Furthermore, we have seen that it also considers the losses achieved than the profits made.

We also discovered that by self-awareness, one is able to find out his shortcoming and hence aim at finding the right strategy to improve rather than becoming emotional and making hasty reactions.

We have also seen that successful traders are never quitters, but instead, they are persistent and sober in their minds. They are very humble in their operations and always seeks to understand more than what they know. They have a teachable spirit.

We hope that you enjoyed this topic and other related topics. Aim at becoming a better swing trader which others can emulate

Chapter 7: Ideal Strategies for Swing Trading Options

This is an uncomplicated strategy that aims at generating quick and secure returns. This strategy has got three significant benefits, namely:

- The excellent opportunity to experience remarkable returns on an initial investment
- The right swing-trading options will limit potential risks
- It is possible to trade high-priced stocks on a small-account

If you are to trade a small trading-account, your initial investment can be leveraged through the application of the options for swing trading strategy. You do not need a substantial capital investment like trading expensive stocks, i.e. Amazon and others.

This strategy focuses on puts and calls options. In this case, if you want to purchase stock, you will buy call-options, or if you wanted a more advanced means of selling a stock, you would have to purchase put-options.

Why We Choose Options for Swing-Trading

One reason that makes this strategy potential over other strategies is the factor of high-profit margin. Everyone expects huge profit margins after trading; for that reason; the best channel to those best profits is this swing trading for options strategy.

This strategy is safe and secure. We are going to explore in details the real principles which make this strategy the best choice for you for profit-making.

Call-Buy Options

As we will see later, swing trading options strategy consists of six steps that are applicable to any market. They are referred to as swing trading options. These are simple but essential principles that can guide you to understand options trading and how best you can relate with a swing-trading options strategy.

1. Picking The correct Stock

When dealing with options for swing trading, the first principle is to ensure that you go in for the right stock. This is because there are vast stocks mentioned on the market for stock exchange, especially in the New York stocks exchange ready for trading.

The main objective here is to develop a robust sector-watch list that contains the leading-stocks.

On your watch list, you are supposed to wait for outside as well as the largest percentage-moves before using these stocks to execute the swing trading-options strategy.

If the bigger-percentage move is for some earning reports that have got an active catalyst, then that is much better because it signifies that there are stronger primary reasons driving stock prices.

2. You Need To Do A Market Environment Assessment

For a case where you wish to buy calls, you need to wait for a bullish trend. It is so good to establish the type of market you are in, to effectively trade the right swing trading options.

As long as you know the market you are in, you will be able to define the right side of the trade you can be either short or long.

If you want to establish the bullish trends, what you need to do, is to find out a series of higher-highs as well as the higher-lows. After defining the patterns of your market, it is essential to evaluate the behaviours of your market environments.

By evaluating the market environment, you may compare characteristics like low-high volatility, which in the long run, will enable you to identify expiration dates for your options for swing trading.

3. You Need To Select Your Strike Price

This is the next step to go for in swing trading options strategy. You must identify the strike price because this can pose a tough job, especially if you do not know how to go about it. In particular, what your aim is, it to identify an option that is out of the money but not so far from out of the money but goes into-the-money.

When we talk about out of the money option, we mean an option but mostly a call option that has a strike price higher than the market price of an underlying asset. On the other hand, it can also be a put option which has its strike price lower than the market price of an underlying asset.

4. Select The Expiration For Options

An optimal strategy must allow enough time for your stock to go through the strike price for it to yield profits on the call options else it could end up expiring worthlessly. You need to bear in mind that if your expiration is very big, in one way, it reduces the risk as the percentage gain come s down respectively.

When you buy call options, you need to embrace an entry tactic of buying pullbacks. It is also essential to establish a maxim stop-loss order shortly after you buy the option and then organize your take profit at a place where you presume the market shall be before the expiry date.

5. Trade management.

You will want to reduce the positions at times when there is low volatility as you continue with sing trading options strategy.

In general, swing trading options strategy is a very powerful option for sing trading. However, you also need to be knowledgeable about how to use it before you apply it.

As earlier discussed, swing trading is a type of trading where; you hold the stocks for just a short period off time. This is different from day trading in that, in day trading you hold stocks for some time before you release them the same day, but for swing trading, the stocks can be held for a period of two days to two weeks.

The main reason for holding stocks for too long is so that you can make more profits from them with time. Prices change with time, so the traders capitalize on the swinging or changing of the costs to achieve more profits. That is where the name 'swing' trade comes from.

In swing trading options strategy, you only need to commit to the trade if your desires are achieved. It is well if you received a down payment or advance to your stocks. The fact remains that you need to work strictly in time frames specified else you risk losing your initial investment.

However, since you did not invest fully, you will not get the total loss. This makes swing trading with options a great strategy since it leverages your initial capital.

When you exercise trading options trading, you gain the option to buy and sell at a later stage based on specific criteria in a specified time frame. You will either work with a put option or call option basing on whether you are buying or selling.

Profitability Chart

You need to define a profitability chart that will aid you in determining some factors for your success. There are issues that you need to consider in a profitability chart that e shall be discussing briefly below.

Consider Moving-Averages

To determine support and resistance levels in the trade, you need to consider moving averages. They are also responsible for defining the present market environmental conditions. There are however, two types of moving averages to find in this context:

a. Simple Moving Average or SMA.

It helps in determining the present climatic condition of the markets. Whether it is bullish or bearish, as well you can be able to define resistance or support levels at this point. Furthermore, you can learn price points that usually help you to know when to enter or exit the trade.

b. Exponential Moving Averages or EMA

This is the second type of moving averages that you need to know and understand. EMA is much concerned with trend signals. Trends can help you to define your entry and exit points. It can also aid you when drawing your business plans.

Float

When you hear about float, it means the total number of shares existing on the market for public trading. They greatly influence you in deciding the right investment plan for you. However, you need to differentiate with shares outstanding. The figure is inclusive of restricted shares.

There is a great challenge when it comes to massive floats. It makes it very difficult for stocks to move in profitable ways. O the other hand, stocks which have small shares supply, can easily display more striking movement.

When you deal with a low float, there is a lot of restraint in movement. Suppose a stock is not traded highly, it won't be able to get the expected move.

Short Interest

When you understand a short interest, it is possible to widen your knowledge before entering the swing trading. The interest is a ratio used to compare the number of floating shares with shares short.

In most cases, short interest is calculated monthly; however, there is no specific source for such data. There is a lot of guesswork done at this very level and also includes the shares which were sold short.

Is it so Important?

In case of high short interest, the chances are that the market could be trending towards bearish with such stock. On the other hand, if the stock is low priced and has got a high short-interest, it serves as a warning of the occurrence of the short squeeze.

If a stock has got a high short-interest which could be cross-referenced using a positive a catalyst, it gives a sign that the short sellers are hoping to be self-covered which finally may negatively affect the price of the stocks.

Volatility

Volatility in stock markets signifies risks. When you hear of risks, it implies that there are chances of making losses in the trades.

It is imperative to consider volatility in swing trading for it is the liability-to-change unpredictably and fast towards the worse. Risking does not necessarily lead to losses; instead it could be a basis for making higher profits. Business is risking, so whatever you gain from trade in some ratio, is proportional to the level of your risking.

Swing trading with options also entails trading with pullbacks. Let us explore this type of trading and see how suitable it is for you.

Pullbacks

A pullback is simply the movement of the prices against the prevailing trend. When we talk about trading-pullbacks in trends, we will be entering the trend direction. This means that the markets have traded at lower prices.

This is a fundamental strategy which follows the trends in trades. You can benefit from trading pullbacks in many ways and in all time-frames.

One of the advantages of trading pullbacks in trends is that you buy low and sell high. When you trade pullbacks in an uptrend, means that you are buying low. When you sell pullbacks in a downtrend, you will be selling high.

Another advantage is its simplicity psychologically. This is as a result of the trends working out for you.

There are indicators that you need to achieve the trading strategy that includes pullbacks.

Fibonacci Retracement Indicator

This works with the Fibonacci ratios, which are essential in determining the resistance and support levels from the point of price reversal.

As you trade pullbacks in trends, the best levels of Fibonacci range from 38.2, 50, and 61.8 percent. It usually comes back to the trend strength and the margin at which the pullback can go.

If the trend is active, the pullback shall be small.

Rules of Trading Pullback Strategy

We need to know the laws that apply when we are trading with pullbacks. These are the same as how we can profit from trading pullbacks. Yes, it is possible to gain a lot from withdrawals as a way of swing trading with options trading.

1. Buying opportunities

There secrete of this trading strategy lies in the fact that we are trading in the trend direction as we enter on a pullback. This gives you more opportunities for gaining profits by limiting the risks of lose. If you wish to profit most from trading pullbacks, it is essential to define the trading trend.

If we do that, it will become easy to trade with trends alone to achieve much profit.

Step 1: Establish a Bullish Trend

This is a trend that comprises of high-highs as well as high-lows only. Identification of the trends should be an easy procedure to you. You can use the swing high versus the low structure. For the case of an uptrend, you will find high-highs as well as high lows respectively thus HH and HL as in the figure below:

Recall: It is quite vital to use higher-time frames to draw the trends. It doesn't matter the time frames that you are used to in determining your trade trends.

Step 2: Adjust To One-Hour Time-Frame and Trace Your Pullback against up trends

Now that you have identified the trend successfully, it is easier to switch lower to the time-frame you prefer most. This is the most preferred time frame, as you may feel well. It could be any time frame, but as for this trading strategy, we will prefer the one-hour time frame.

After that, we need to figure out the trade entry point. This is where the real trading strategy comes in.

Step 3: Put the "FRI" Between the Previous Swing Low and High Levels before the Pullback

You need to consider the previous swing high and low. After that, position your Fibonacci Retracement Indicator amid the swings. This is as indicated in the chart below:

After doing all that, you need to know precisely at what level you will be joining the trade.

Step 4: Consider Buying Anywhere within the Fibonacci Retracement Area, i.e. (50-61.8) %.

You need to place a Fibonacci retracement mark on the chart at an area that is underlying in the rates of 50-61.8 per cent. Then, you will have to determine the exact place where you will execute the buying process. You can decide to buy soon as it hits the 50 percent mark or even wait till it hits the 61.8 percent mark.

As you go on with this business, you gain more knowledge and experience, which helps you to determine the possible entry and exit points to the trade and possible mechanisms of making much profit.

We are now in trade. Thus we need to find ways in which we can fix or hide stop-loss orders.

Step 5: Fix Protective Stop-Loss Order Right under the Swing-Low

At the previous swing low, we can hide our protective stop-loss order there. This is the best place to implement our stop-loss. A break right below the last most swing-low can cancel off the trade. So it is good if we reduced losses as we exit the trade.

It is important to devise a proper strategy of maximizing profits as we trade pullbacks. This leads us to the next strategy.

Step 6: Collect Profit Soon As You Break Above the Last Swing-High

There should be a strategy for picking profits for us to benefit from trading pullbacks. As soon as we reach a new high, this is the best place to exit the trade as we make our profits. A point to note is that markets never move in straight lines.

In many cases, after breaking to new highs, we expect a pullback to occur suddenly. For you to be either in or out of the market easily is the best way to realize profits from pullbacks.

On the other hand, we can maximize our profits by taking only half of our profits as soon as we break to new highs. The remaining bit of the profits should be taken after it reaches one hundred percent of the Fibonacci extension.

How Much Profits Can Be Expected?

As long as you are swing trading with options strategy, there is a definite outcome that you need to expect. However just alike any business out there, the expectations are never inevitable. This is because e of the volatility of this type of trade. We have considered many factors which influence the nature of the profits that can be obtained.

As we said earlier, the nature of returns is entirely dependent on the trader himself. If you compared for example trading leveraged ETF's with stock trading, you find that some will yield well as others back fire.

The approach taken in this case is also a key factor to consider. Basing on the strategy applied, some traders will go praising their returns as others weep over the loss.

For example some may opt for candle-sticks charts with support & resistance levels whereas others will opt for news.

The only trick in this case is to establish the rightful strategy that works well for you. However much it may be different from day trading, swing trading with options strategy may be the most effective strategy especially for people with less or no experience.

This is because, day trading involves thousands of securities to deal in therefore can be very cumbersome. As for swingers, they will experience their returns after two days w which makes them more motivate than the days' traders.

At the same time, wing trading is short term compared options trading. This makes the traders to realize profits earlier to eliminate distraction.

Learning how to trade with swings is fairly straightforward however the capital is set at risk. Because of such reason, there should be a lot of caution to be taken at all times.

Right Market

There are two typical market set ups where swing trading can be exercised. The bear market and the raging bull market. Depending on the market selected, even the active stocks may not portray the same swings as for the indices which are stable for quite some time.

You will find that for the case of bull or bear market, momentum usually carries stocks for relative periods yet in one given direction. This implies that the best strategies as well as entry points lie on longer term trends.

Therefore, it is only until the markets are headed nowhere is when you it is the right time for swing trading arena.

Chapter 8: Swing Trading Examples

Swing trading is a very profitable business. With the right knowledge and intentions, you can easily succeed in this trading style. This chapter discusses a few examples of swing trading stocks and options.

Whether you wish to trade options, stocks or other financial instruments, it is important that you always establish whether the opportunity presented is right for a swing trade. You are supposed to enter only those trades that have the potential to generate positive results. The following are some of the signs that indicate a favorable trading position.

- The direction of the market is moving according to your expectation. When you want to purchase stock or options, ensure that the market has assumed a stable uptrend. If you wish to sell then ensure that the market will assume a downtrend in future.
- The industry associated with a particular stock is also acting according to your expectations. Most stock prices tend to fluctuate depending on the industry they are derived. If the industry is doing

well, there is a high possibility of making profit from the related stocks.

- In case you wish to trend trade, ensure that you make a purchase as soon as a technical signal or breakout occurs. If you wish to trade ranges, you must be able to identify support and resistance levels early enough. Watch out for any signals, crossovers and divergence to ensure that you maximize you profits.

- There is correlation between technical and fundamental factors of a particular stock. Use your trading charts to identify some fundamental catalysts. Check out for important catalysts and see if these coincide with the technical aspects of the market.

- When the stop-loss of the stock is close to the target price. The best stocks from swing trading are the ones that feature emergency exit points. The closer the entry price gets to the stop-loss price the less amount of capital you lose in each trade. You should always consider exiting the market at this point since you will save yourself from further losses. However, check out for stocks whose stop-loss price is not too close to the stock price. Such stocks always end too quickly into the trade.

- The amount you need to trade has been set right. Swing trading is always associated with so many uncertainties. Get into positions that are compatible with your trading plan and routine. Do not compromise your strategies to suit your emotions. Have a limit to your position sizes and amount of capital invested.

Examples

1. Bullish Breakout Swing Trade

This example is based on trend trading. The market prices have been increasing steadily for over two months. However, in the past few days, the stock pattern has backtracked from a previous resistance levels.

The trader identified a breakout entry above the previous support level and confirmed that a resistance had occurred recently at $7.55. The trader thus set the entry price to $7.60. This is illustrated in the figure below:

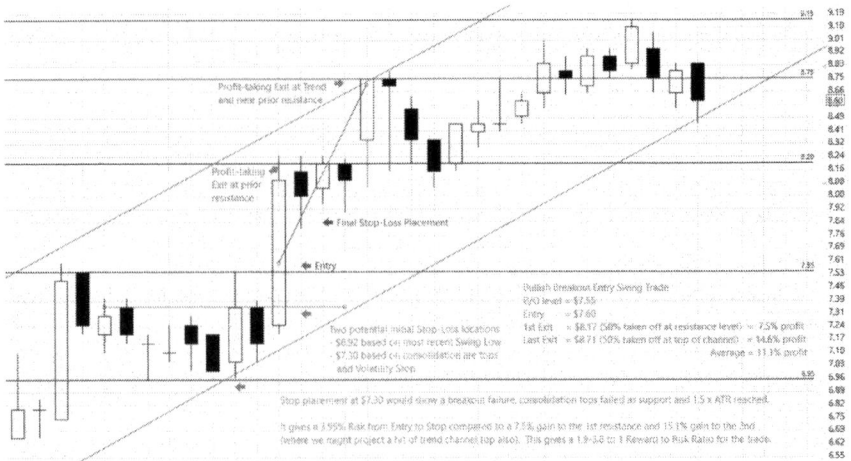

Figure 1: Breakout swing trade

The trader also placed two stop-loss orders below the previous swing low, which is at $6.92. If the stop loss was placed exactly at this point, it would result in a loss of about 9% of the initial capital.

The second stop-loss order was placed under the support line that is drawn at the top of a consolidation that just ended. With a volatility stop that corresponds to the stop price, the ideal point for this order was found to be at $7.30. This meant that if the price of stock gets to $7.30 it would indicate a fail in the existing breakout. It would also mean that the support level located above the just concluded consolidation had not succeeded. Thirdly, this would also mean that the price decline was 1.5 times the stock's volatility rate. With such explanation, it is clear that the trader made a mistake entering in such a position. Thus, he needs to close the position as soon as possible to avoid further loss.

Another possible target in this example is when the trader identifies a resistance level by studying the price pattern for the past two years. It was established by the trader that the last resistance line was at $8.20. However, the price level had experienced numerous reversals in both the uptrend and the downtrend over the two years. Therefore the trader decided to sell when the market is strong, but when the prices are yet to reach the resistance level. He set the target price for closing the position at $8.17. If the market goes according to the trader's expectation, he would take home a profit of 7.5 percent.

The third target is estimated at a price of $8.75. Over the last two years, this price had also been the support and resistance cost at certain points. Additionally, the past bullish swings in the market can help estimate the price of stock. This would indicate whether it would be at the top of the trend line or not.

Fourthly, the trader also used the principal of selling stock in a strong market and set another target cost of

$8.71. In case the stock prices reached this amount, the resultant profit would be 14.6 percent. If the swings continue to become stronger, this would have indicated the best time to end the position and consolidate some profits.

From this trade, you can tell that there are several opportunities for the swing trader to make money. When the price broke out to reach an entry amount of $7.60, the market became active with activity since the stock prices were also changing drastically. Actually, as soon as the trader entered the market, the stock trended highly until when the trader made the first exit. That implies that the first half of the transaction was completed within a few hours of entering the swing trading position.

Once the first price target was attained, the sell order set by the trader got executed and the stop order changed to a relatively higher amount. Although stop orders do not shield you from huge price gaps, they help you to remain orderly in your trades thus minimizing the risks involved in such gaps. Executing a stop order does not cause a transaction to be negative. From this example, the trade would make a profit of 3.85% in case the position gets stopped out. This means that the pressure exerted on the trader fades off as soon as the stop order is executed.

From the figure, you notice that from the entry day, the resistance level remained at $8.20 remained for over three days. The volatility stop, however, increased over the days and the stop loss price also changed to a final amount of $7.84. During the last day of the trade, the stock prices created larger gaps but sold off at a good profit before retaining its previous trend. The last bit of the transaction ended with a price that was more than the initial target price set at $8.71.

Analysis

This example represents a swing trade that ended into good profit within five days. The net gain was 11.1%, which is a good amount for the investor. However the risk involved in the trade was 3.95%. Therefore, the transaction had a risk/ reward ratio of 2.8/1 which is a good potential for profit.

Note that the trade did not involve the use of sophisticated tools. The only evident tools here are trend lines, support and resistance levels and the volatility stop indicator. However complicated the example seems to be, there were no chart patterns, moving averages nor signals used to predict the market and stock price trends. Although professional traders make a lot more in terms of profit when it comes to swing trading, 11% over five days is a good way to start your swing trading business. Depending on the amount of capital you invested in the trade, this can translate into very good profit amounts.

11.1% of profit over five days means that the trader got an average of 2.2% profit each day. If the trader would have involved the use of charts and other tools in the business, the profits would have been higher. In case this was a long-term position and the market remained consistent for a whole year, the trader would have pocketed a profit of 230%. Since the swing market always features unpredictable changes, it is always not advisable to take too long before claiming profit from positions.

2. The Bearish Consolidated Swing Trade

The first example comprises of a bullish swing trade. This second example focuses on a bearish trade.

A bearish market is one where prices have assumed a consistent downtrend. This means that the prices on the market are expected to decrease in future. As a swing trader, you will always come across bearish stocks and trade signals. When market trends are bearish, it means that they are governed by less buyers and more sellers.

In this example, the trader identifies a stock whose price has been going down over many months. The stock has assumed a constant support line for over a week as indicated in the figure below.

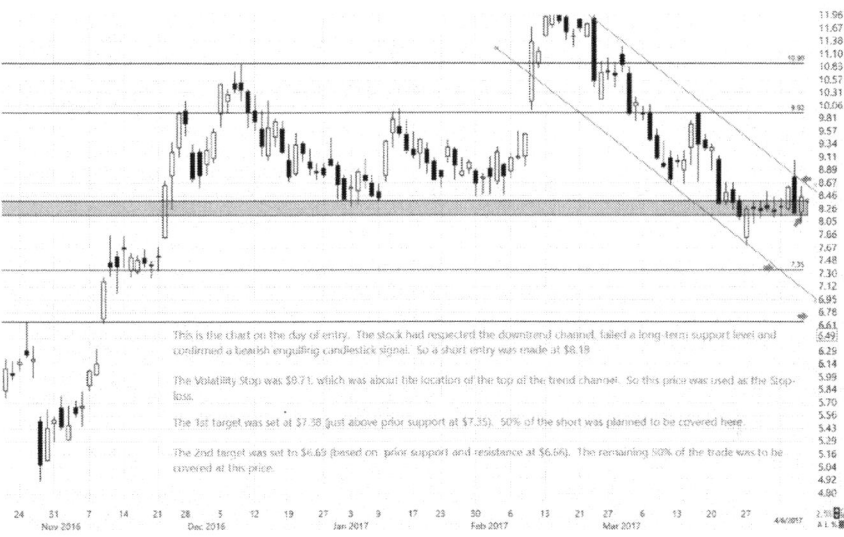

Figure 2: Bearish swing trade example

The sustained support level resulted in a bearish signal that clearly outlined it at the end of the first day. The following day, the prices continued to change downwards, giving the trader the confidence that the bearish signal received was not fake. Thus the trader made a short entry at $8.18. He then used this to create a stop loss order at $8.71 which meant that the position should close once this amount is reached by the market. In case the market declined to assume this price, the trader would have made a loss of 6.48 percent of his initial capital.

The trader then set the initial target price to $7.38, an amount that was slightly higher than the current support level. The support level read at $7.35 and had been assumed by the stock for two years. In case the stock price reached this amount, the trader would have made a profit of 9.78 percent. The goal of the trader was to trade half of the position at this support price than move the stop loss order below this amount in case the target price is attained.

He set the second target cost at $6.69, an amount that was slightly beyond the previous support and resistance level assumed by the market for the past two years. With this target cost, the trader would make a profit of 18.22 percent in case the market works in his favor. The second target was set to cater for the second half of the swing trade position as a way of maximizing the profits associated with the trade.

In case the stock prices hit both target, the trader would proudly walk away with a profit of 14 percent, which is a good amount for most investors. The reward/ risk ratio would stand at 2.16/1. One advantage of this example is that the swing trader got into the market early in the morning when opportunities were still many. The market performed well at the start. However, as the day progressed it turned against the trader but resumed the downward price movement the following day.

The market hit the first price target five days later when the volatility stop had reduced to $7.85. This meant that in case the stock prices reversed at this point, the trader would still make a profit unless huge gaps occurred. The success of the trade had already been guaranteed by day 5. Afterwards the volatility stop reduced again to $7.60 and two day later, the stock price hit the second target covering the entire short position.

From this example, you can clearly see that the bearish market yielded an average profit of 1.75% each day for the short position entered by the trader. This results in an excellent reward/ risk ratio of 2/1.

As a swing trader therefore, you can utilize both bullish and bearish markets to generate profits from your trades. These market types occur whether you are trading stocks, options or other financial instruments. The secret lies in identifying where to set your target, entry and stop loss prices.

Chapter 9: A Day in the Life of a Swing Trader

Swing trading is among the best trading styles for both new and well established traders. If you are just starting off, you can make profit from this strategy as soon as you start using it. Once you begin, you can start enjoying some good returns within a day or two. This is what motivates most people into engaging in the trade.

The strategy involves identifying trending stocks, then placing several short-term transactions against these stocks. The purpose is to purchase and sell stock as close to the upper and lower sings as possible. Successful swing trading requires a lot of dedication and time. You must be ready to research and apply whatever you have learnt to become good at the business. This chapter describes a typical day in the life of a swing trader in terms of setting goals, objectives and routines.

Swing Trading Goals

Swing trading comprises of very unique goals. Most of these revolve around making profit. However, traders who make it using this style always focus on developing winning goals and strategies. When it comes to swing trading, the passion for success is not enough. There are several aspects that you need to put in place to manage the constantly changing market environment.

When you set your trading goals, you must always be ready to adjust them accordingly. Despite having the right goals and strategies in place, adapting to change is a must since market performance may sometimes change abruptly. By adjusting to this change, it does not mean that you get rid of your trading plans and goals completely. It only means that you must understand when to act and when to go slow. It also means that you must beware of opportunities that need quick action and those that do not.

Having good strategies in place is very essential. However, you must not follow these strategies blindly since you may end at a loss. Always understand how to apply each strategy that you have. This also applies to goal setting. Your goals should not focus on making money alone. Instead, they should concentrate on building the trading process. Most traders, especially novice swing traders, develop their goals around numbers. Although this works for a good number of them, some get tied into unprofitable processes and end up losing a lot of capital. When you concentrate on making money as a goal, you will get frustrated each time you experience a loss. That is why you need to concentrate on the process more than the results. If the process is tailored well, the results will be instant. Even if you define the results but the process is weak, no achievement will come forth.

As you work towards achieving your goals, be sure to have a winning plan as well. Every business starts with a business plan. Swing trading is also a form of business that needs an excellent plan. A good plan always defines how you will enter and exit trades as well as how you intend to manage your capital and profits. It should bear every detail about your ideal market, preferred stocks as well as the risks associated with the business. You also need to define the kind of indicators, charts and signals that you wish to use.

When setting your trading plan, it should also entail some information on market environments that you need to avoid. When you focus on making money too much, you may end up getting into positions that are not too promising. Getting out of such positions is always too difficult. You need to learn not to force profits when opportunities are not present. There are times when prices move sideways instead of assuming either an upward or downward trend. You need to avoid such markets since they can easily erode your capital.

Always seek to keep your plan and goals as simple as possible. Some traders think that the more complicated a trading plan is, the more the profit. However, this is never the case. If you complicate your goals and plans too much, you may fail to identify the right strategies to meet these goals. Stick to analysis and trading tools that you understand well. You also need to concentrate on stocks that you have some good knowledge about. Start with a few essential strategies and build on them over time. This will ensure that your performance keeps improving and that you do not engage in any careless activities on the market.

As you apply your plans and strategies, you must also bear in mind that not all trades are the same. Some trades involve highly volatile stocks that feature huge swings while others involve very little movement. You must be ready to act based on every market situation.

Here are some general considerations that you need to make:

- Decide whether to trade on random types of stocks, or whether you need to come up with a predefined list of stocks that meet your trading requirements
- Estimate the amount of capital you intend to risk
- Outline the techniques you want to use to enter and exit trades
- Specify the amount of time you need before you can enter into the business
- Also outline how you will get out of trades and how you intend to use your profits

Swing Trading Objectives

Swing trading objectives are always different from day trading and trend trading objectives. The objective of day traders is to open and close positions in the same day. The aim of long-term trading is to buy stocks and hold onto them for a long period so as to sell them at a profit. You can invest in swing trading by yourself or with the help of a broker.

Due to the relatively short-term nature of swing trading, there are some basic rules that you need to abide by. These are as outlined below:

- If you time your entry points correctly, you may start earning some profit from the trade as soon as you enter the market. If the timing is wrong, you might start losing immediately

- Exit the market as soon as you realize that it is not performing according to your expectations

- When the market direction moves in favor of your strategy, allow it to go overnight and only exit as soon as there is an indication of a change of direction. Sometimes overnight trades offer the best opportunities to generate income from swing trading. Be flexible with your entry and exit times since these must not be the same for every stock that you trade

- Once you make your target profits, go slow in entering other opportunities

- Always focus on minimizing the risks. Do not trade when you are not sure about the direction the market might take in future

- Although it is possible to recover a losing trade, never allow a losing position to remain open throughout the night. You should exit the market and start over the next day

Routine of a Swing Trader

The biggest difference between expert and losing swing traders lies in how the two manage their routine. Professional traders always transact using clear routines which maximize the number of opportunities they get each week. Average and non-performing traders often enter positions by luck, not knowing whether they will make a profit or loss from their trades. A good routine helps you to improve your swing trading results. It also ensures that you do not waste your time engaging in unnecessary trading activities.

For an average swing trader, the strategy can sometimes become difficult due to lack of the right experience and information. Here is an outline of how a typical day in your life as a swing trader needs to look like.

Pre-market

This is the period before you enter the market. Mostly it starts in the morning at 6:00 am until the swing market opens for the day. How you spent this time determines the amount of profit you get at the end of your swing trades. This is always the right time to identify the right opportunities to trade. It is also the time you need to come up with a watch list and check out how your existing open positions performed overnight. The premarket hour entails the following activities:

1. *Overview of the market* – this is also done as soon as you start your swing trading session. You need to check out some of the factors that may influence price fluctuations on the market by updating yourself on the latest news and events in the swing market. You can get this information from reputable financial news channels as well as websites. When doing this check out for the overall market sentiments such as whether the market is bearish or bullish, changes in currency rates, economic reports as well as the occurrence of inflation in the market. You should also look out for sector related sentiments which outline some of the best sectors to trade in for the day. Finally, get to check out the performance of the underlying companies associated with the financial instruments you wish to swing trade.

2. *Creating a watch list* - a watch list is a list of the kind of swing trading opportunities you wish to engage in during the trading session. Most of a swing trader's watch list is often made up of stocks that have a fundamental catalyst tied to them. Some traders always have a board next to them where they note the kind of opportunities they wish to trade in terms of the entry, exit and stop-loss costs.

3. *Identifying trades* – once you have understood about what to expect on the market, the next thing you should do is research the best trades for the trading period of your choice. Most swing traders always enter positions that are capable to change prices significantly during the trading period. They always prefer stocks that have a fundamental catalyst attached to them since these have a higher potential of moving prices in the future. Fundamental catalysts are often categorized in two ways – special opportunities and sector plays. Special opportunities include things like initial public offerings, buyouts, mergers and acquisitions as well as takeovers and headline news. Although such opportunities bear a high level of risk, they also

carry a very large profit potential should the market work in the trader's favor.

Sector plays comprise of things such as company financial information as well as changes in the sector of trade. For instance, if your stock is derived from the energy sector and there is an announcement that the sector is scheduled to improve in the next few days, there will be a significant change in the prices of your stock.

4. *Monitoring the existing positions* – this is a continuous activity carried out any time of the day. It is important to do this so as to identify the positions you need to close and those that should remain open. The decision to close or open positions is often determined by the information you receive in the morning about the market performance. You can always find information about a certain stock position by typing the stock symbol in a search engine and getting to the news section. Check for anything that may impact your trading plan as well, then adjust your stop-loss strategies accordingly.

Trading Hours

This refers to the real market hours where you engage in the trade. After studying the market and understanding its attributes for the day, you should now focus on carrying out the right transactions. Visit the market maker and find out what they have in stock since these stocks are known to perform well most of the time. Beware of fake bid and ask prices presented by some unreliable traders since these can get you into trouble.

As soon as you identify a potential trading opportunity, start working on an exit plan to ensure that you safeguard any profits that you make from the trade. You can do this by the use of technical indicators. Some traders set exit plans way before placing a trade while others wait until they get into the market.

After-market Hours

This is the period after you are done with your swing trading session. It is a time to reflect on your transactions, not a time to place more trades. When you use this time correctly, you will be able to identify the mistakes made during the trade and how to avoid them. You do this by going through the activities of each trade and identifying those things you need to change.

From this routine, it is clear that having the right routine is crucial for swing trading success. This is the time when you get to plan your day and all its activities. It is essential that you plan your day well to ensure that market hours are only set aside for trading. Once you adapt to a routine, you will notice significant improvement in most of your trading sessions

Printed in Great Britain
by Amazon